Speaking of Trust
Conversing with Luther
about the Sermon on the Mount

Speaking of Trust
Conversing with Luther
about the Sermon on the Mount

Martin E. Marty

Augsburg Fortress
Minneapolis

SPEAKING OF TRUST
Conversing with Luther about the Sermon on the Mount

Editor: Scott Tunseth

Cover Design: Koechel Peterson and Associates, Inc., Minneapolis, MN
www.koechelpeterson.com

Cover photo: Koechel Peterson and Associates, Inc., Minneapolis, MN

ISBN 0-8066-4994-1

The paper used in this publication meets the minimum requirements of American National Standard for Information Sciences—Permanence of Paper for Printed Library Materials, ANSI Z329.48-1984.

Manufactured in the U.S.A.

07   06   05   04   03   1   2   3   4   5   6   7   8   9   10

Contents

Introduction 7

1. A Lesson from the Birds and the Flowers! 24

2. Seek First the Kingdom 39

3. Ask 55

4. When You Pray 63

5. The Lord's Prayer 76

6. Blessed Are You 92

7. Hungering for Justice 114

8. Pure-hearted Peacemakers 125

9. In the Company of the Persecuted 142

Editor's Note

In 1983, Harper and Row (San Francisco) published a book entitled *The Place of Trust*. That book, which is now out of print, included a brief introduction by Martin E. Marty and selected portions of Luther's commentary on The Sermon on the Mount taken from *Luther's Works*, Volume 21 (translated by Jaroslav Pelikan), © 1956 by Concordia Publishing House.

In this volume, *Speaking of Trust*, Marty revisits this same material from Luther on The Sermon on the Mount in a new and greatly expanded way. The new Introduction has doubled in size, and Marty has added his conversation with Luther in each of the book's nine chapters. Questions for individual and group reflection have also been added so that readers can carry on their own conversation with the two "Martins" and with the timeless text of Matthew's Gospel.

Introduction

By Martin E. Marty

We are in on this conversation about trust together. I make bold to represent you. Then I bid you to pass on its words of grace and trust to others, since they join us in being in this together.

Do you find those lines a bit presumptuous, even offensive, since I took you for granted? I wrote them in the hope that they would engage you and perhaps arouse you to be suspicious and maybe a bit resentful. Now I hope in a few paragraphs to allay the suspicion, minimize the possible resentment, and invite you to an adventure that can be positive. If successful, these lines will leave us unburdened and unself-conscious so that we can better hear the words of Matthew's Gospel and of commentator Martin Luther, and then choose our own means and mode of responding.

There are good reasons for readers to resent headline writers, or writers in general, who take them for granted with the use of the word "we." Thus a magazine cover will say something like "Why We Are All Into Collectibles" or "Why We Are Avoiding Vacations in France" or "Why We Christians Are 'Into' Contemporary Worship."

Wait! there is an impulse to say. "I am not into collectibles or out of France or committed to only one form of worship." Or: "How do you know what I am 'into'? Did you ask me? Did you take a poll? If I am not part of your 'we' am I a dissenter, an eccentric, an individualist, a maverick, a nut? Why did you presume to speak for me? Am I better off to find myself included in the pack of people about whom you are generalizing, or are you implying I would be better off not collecting collectibles, avoiding France, or cherishing other-than-contemporary worship forms? In general the message to writers has to be: "Handle 'we' and 'us' and 'our' with care!"

Having uttered all those words of caution, this writer—dare I say "I" in a book that is going to be about "us" and "we"?—is going to be incautious, reckless, free about inferring that reader and writer are in the boat of life together. That we sometimes find ourselves "in over our heads." That we rejoice in some of the same victories, experience similar disappointments and defeats. That we care about our eternal destiny and, somehow, hope to be found in the gracious keeping of a loving God.

Being incautious in a book on spirituality allows us to do something that the author of half this book, Martin Luther, commended: "Sin boldly." That is an often misused and easily misusable line. Some might find it a license to do bad stuff. But those who read and listen to the whole paragraph can find a context in which it makes sense. Picture me, the writer, here being what Luther called "a preacher of grace," which is something anyone can be who experiences and proclaims the grace of God. Read on:

> If you are a preacher of grace, then preach a true and not a fictitious grace; if grace is true, you must bear a true and not fictitious sin. God does not save people who are only fictitious sinners. Be a sinner and sin boldly, but believe and rejoice in Christ even more boldly, for he is victorious over sin, death, and the world." (H. Lehman, ed. *Luther's Works*, Fortress, 48: 281-282.)

To apply this to the present point: readers have a right to privacy, a freedom to make up their own minds, to choose their own attitudes, to speak for themselves. Yet they are also called to take part in company and communion with others, in the trail of a gospel which assumes that there are some constant features in human life and a Savior who has a word to address them.

In reach of the gospel

What am I here assuming about us, the "we" of this book?

First, that we are all somehow in reach of the gospel. Of course, atheists or people of other faiths are welcome to read the book, and they may find that at many points it talks about common human stories, hopes, and fears. But they will stand outside the rang- what the Gospel, Luther's comment, and my part of the conversation assume: some sort of faith in God, some understanding that the good news of God in the gospel speaks to their situation.

The next assumption about "us"—it's time to throw away the quotation marks around the pronouns, so let me try it again. The next assumption about us is that the routines of ordinary life often keep us from being alert to the signals God gives, when we are asked to put trust in God. If ordinariness does not dull us, setbacks distract us. When the "big D's" of Doubt, Disappointment, or Depression, anything this side of utter Despair, afflict us, as they sooner or later will, the whole idea of putting trust in God gets clouded.

To face up to these distractions and traumas, we listen to Scriptures and comment upon them. Curiously, faith grows as we talk about it to others and listen to them. Luther himself admitted that he did not have as much faith as others thought he had, nor did the apostle Paul, but that he grew confident when he did think about it and talk about it. He thought the same was true of Paul, who also provided many clues about his own inner struggles over faith. I have nothing magical in mind here; one does not move from unfaith to faith by chattering, nor do away with doubt by covering it up through dialogue. Yet the experience of strugglers and saints through the ages is clear: bring to mind and tongue both the problems of the inner life and the word of God's promise to deal with them, and you will find life transformed.

A third assumption about us is that we humans need help. Martin Luther liked to use a Latin word to describe our problem. Try it on for size. He says the human is *incurvatus in se*. You do not need to know Latin to get a clue; the word "curve" is tucked into the phrase. Yes, the human is "curved in" upon himself or herself. Try an experiment to test this feature of life. Read the morning papers for gross examples: sometimes the financial pages will tell stories of successes by the proud. We used to say of such: "He is a self-made man who worships his creator." Sometimes the sports pages will focus on an individual who is convinced she made it on her own, owes nothing to anyone, can choose her lifestyle without regard for the common good. We say she is "full of herself." Not to discriminate: the religion pages can have as many such examples as any other.

Curved in and self-enclosed

Continue the experiment: visit with others and invite them to cast their cares away, preferably to the place where God acts, to the depth of the heart where God reaches. Then ask whether they still worry, and, if so, why they do so? Probably their guard is still up: they have to take care of themselves, build defenses around themselves, and not be open to the risk that comes with trusting others, trusting God. I cheated in that paragraph: among the "others" is "the self." Which means that the place to look for what it means to be curved in upon one's self is the mirror, or the door of access to the heart and soul. One asks: "Am I so 'curved in' upon myself that I cannot be open to God's promise, assurance, and grace? Am I curled up, self-enclosed, protective, looking out only for the way I can take care of me?"

Let me interrupt this little exercise with an apology or an explanation. If you are like me, you don't like to be condescended to, to have someone unauthorized to do so, to play a schoolmaster-like role and explain what does not look as if it needs explanation. What we are talking about in both the Latin phrase that went before and the one that follows belongs to the category of "What I already know." I have read somewhere that the task of the teacher is to try to discern what a student already knows, to get him or her to overcome whatever it is that represses this knowledge or the use of such knowledge, and then to hope the student will act upon it. Which is why the teacher asks most of the questions.

I am stepping aside with this little language lesson both to those who know what is in it already and those who do not because it is very important that we understand each other at the beginning of the pilgrimage we are going to take. So the music teacher makes sure that everyone who is going to sing or play understands the musical notation, or the flight trainer goes over the dashboard dials with even experienced students who have flown other craft. End of apology.

If you buy the assumption that we are all curved in upon ourselves and not naturally open to the surprising work of God, the next thing is to ask why that is the case. Another way to put that is: what is it about human nature that keeps those of us who are baptized believers from accepting the benefits of baptism and the yields of belief? Here once again I am going to draw upon a term of Martin Luther, who has a right to be cited often, since this is his book. He deduced something from the writings of the apostle Paul, other biblical witnesses, and great Christian thinkers before him, and he came up with a formula: The human is *simul justus et peccator.*

Once again, I beg for patience if you do not read Latin or find italicized foreign words smuggled into English texts rather off-putting. This one, too, explains itself, is memorable, and includes an astonishing observation. The *simul* is easy; we know it from words like "simultaneous" or "simulcast." It alerts us to the idea that we can be at the same time two apparently independent and even contradictory beings. *Justus* signals being declared just by God. This is at the heart of Paul's and Luther's proclamation: God in Christ took pains, even to the pain of the cross, to effect what Luther called a "joyful exchange." We bring our sins, and God declares us just because of Christ's sacrifice. Christ brings his holiness, perfection, and Godhead and exchanges situations with us, suffering in identification with sinners.

As for the word *peccator*, we find it in words like "peccadilloes," which are little bitty sins, petty offenses, things we can pretty well take care of on our own. But the *peccator* is a full-blooded, full-blown, fully engaged sinner, the top-to-bottom errant person who is in real trouble. In some versions of the Christian faith the believer is a kind of climber into the good graces of God. In that case, at each rung of the ladder of achievement or the steps of merits gained, the climber progresses, leaving behind more and more of the errant being she or he was. Wrong. Of course, there is "growth in grace," and of course, believers along the way get to realize ever more the reach of a merciful God. But with growth in grace there is also growth of temptation. In the old language, the graced believer is ever greater game for the enemies of God, beginning with the devil.

The reality that we are "at the same time declared just and remaining sinners" means that when God looks at the believer "in Christ," God sees Christ, with all his virtues and benefits. When God looks at the believer apart from Christ and from faith in Christ, God sees the sinful human.

Looking at all the saints who ever lived, all the sinners ever rescued throughout history, and looking around us at everyone we know, or looking within at the one we know best, we find that the *peccator* side is there. Looking at the record of saints, rescued sinners, and the saved self, we find the *justus* side. At the same time. So in this book we will assume that all believing readers are sinners and people made just, and that the words of Luther on which we comment take for granted both the human needs and the human hungers that go with such experience.

With these two understandings of the nature of believers, we also make the assumption that humans all need not only food and drink for the body and shelter over the head and against the storm, but also some measure of security, a healthy sense of self, a set of people to whom one belongs, some affirming strokes along the way, and even some outlets for the service of others.

Conversing with the printed page

Another introductory element has to do with the concept of conversation. This book is advertised as a conversation, and in a way takes on the form of one. Of course, it is not a true dialogue as it would be if we were face to face with each other, or could be one on one with Martin Luther. There is something artificial about the notion of conversing with the printed page. But I am emboldened to think of certain kinds of reading taking on that character.

Machiavelli, not someone I would set forth as an example in most respects, had this one right. He wrote that when he came home from the day's doings, he doffed his dusty or muddy clothes and put on "garments regal and courtly." Why? He was going to converse with his friends. He explained that this meant he was going into his library to open and read the books. There he would be in the company of the great people of the ages. They would impart their knowledge and insight to him and he, in turn, was free to ask questions. They would in their turn, be generous in continuing such a conversation. In other words, not all books are finished products. Most of them beckon the reader to take part, to ask questions, or get ideas to which they would respond. That is what we do in normal human conversation and what we hope will go on here.

Here is something important about the nature of conversation, especially conversation defined over against argument. Some books of religion, theology, and faith are exercises in argument. They set out to prove the existence of God, the truth of the Bible, the rightness or wrongness of doctrine based on the Bible, the value of a proposition about faith. Argument is governed by the answer: I have an answer and I must expound it and then debate you, until—unless you win the argument—I convince you, convert you, humiliate you, or drive you away.

Argument about the meaning of trust and the means of gaining it or receiving it is legitimate. But it is not the present point. Conversation, on the other hand, is governed not by answers but by questions. You never say, at the end, "I sure won that conversation," because conversation is not a contest or a conflict. Conversation is a game, a bidding, an invitation to take part. Here we are assuming that we do not know enough about worry and trust, about doubt and faith, to have all the answers or the ability to put them to work in proper ways. We ask each other, and we will ask Luther, to advance the conversation.

If this works well, the reader of a few pages here and there will less likely say "Now I am convinced" so much as "I never thought of it that way before." Never must she feel that these pages complete or close off the conversation. Instead, one picks it up and passes it on. (I picture the book also used in company, communion, and class, where the provided questions at the end of chapters can inspire and promote further inquiry and conversation.)

Perhaps we slid over the concept that a text is not a finished product, and ought to pause for a moment. You have in your hands a book made up of paper impressed with molecules of ink. Together with some glue to hold the pages together, you have what looks like a finished product. Someone published it, marketed it, and sold it, to you or a library. After it goes out, I have no way of correcting errors in it, of adding paragraphs, especially since I cannot track down everyone who reads it. In that sense, yes, it is a finished product.

In other ways, however, it is open, never complete, not even when you have read it and done your own agreeing or disagreeing with it. Realizing that, we have occasion to ask exactly what such a text sets out to do. The text may be biblical, it may come from Luther, it may be this one. Let's stick with the first of these, the biblical.

Scholars tell us that there are basically three ways of addressing texts. First, they study what one calls "the world behind the text," which is something historians do. Were this book about that, we would be spending our main energies on how the Sermon on the Mount got put together and presented to us. What part might reflect the teaching of rabbis, one of which Jesus was. What elements show that they come out of the Judaism of which Jesus was a part as an heir of the covenant? How did the author of the Gospel of Matthew gather and organize materials to present the sermon. It is no assault on biblical integrity to pay attention to this. We have a "Sermon on the Plain" in Luke to go with this "Sermon on the Mount," and the two possess enough common features that we can find an editorial hand at work.

Now and then a film based on the Bible suggests a situation that cannot have prevailed. I recall a half-century-old film, *Ben Hur*, which portrayed Jesus preaching the Sermon on the Mount. The filmmakers properly based it outdoors, on a mountainside. But they showed worshipers coming to the scene as if it were a suburban church on Sunday morning. They march in neat rows, as if an usher were at hand bidding them to find a pew, in this case grassy ground. They listen reverently. One almost expects a hymn before and after the sermon, and then the collection of offerings. One does not have to be a movie critic or a biblical critic to see that a later age is imposing on an earlier time its view of Jesus' discourse.

Learning as much as we can about what Jesus said, how it got remembered and passed on to a later generation, and how the Gospel of Matthew came to be, enhances our understanding. But in the end that belongs mainly to the classroom, and we are aiming for the heart.

A second way to deal with texts, say the scholars, is to study "the world of the text." This is the task of the literary scholar, a task to which all readers are commended. One can never know too much about what makes up a text or set of texts. It is devastating to read a vision (as in Daniel, Ezekiel, or Revelation) as a newspaper account of something happening. The authors of those books alert readers that they are recording visions, not happenings. It is confusing to read the Psalms as history or the Book of Chronicles as devotional psalms. We have good reason to want to know the form and style of Gospels. What is the "world of the parable" or the allegory, as opposed to the world of reporting? These are very, very important themes for the classroom, and, lifelong, the life of the mind of believers. But it is not what Luther's reading of the Sermon on the Mount and his preaching, which became the text, press on us.

No, third is the option that preoccupies us: "the world in front of (or ahead of) the text." That is, to what understanding and action does this text bid us? Another way to put it: to what does the comment of Luther and, behind it, the words of the Sermon on the

Mount commit us? It is clear that they are bidding us to view the horizon, the future, differently than we would if we just looked ahead naturally. There are no natural reasons to regard the world as anything but indifferent to us, uncaring, ready to let us be forgotten. There are no natural rationales for ending the task of worrying about what we should eat or wear. There are not natural reasons to assume that God answers prayer.

In the Sermon on the Mount the words of Jesus bid us to regard God as overcoming the world's indifference and showing care; call it "supernaturally," not in the sense of magic but of demonstrating divine Lordship and concern. In the Sermon on the Mount, also as Luther reads it, Jesus invokes the character of his Father to give us "superhuman" reasons to do away with worry about tomorrow, though we are allowed to be concerned about the tasks and needs taken up today. In the Sermon on the Mount we are bidden to look at the horizon, the future, differently when we bring those needs to the divine Father in prayer. We would not "naturally" have done any of the above. Jesus reveals a God who is different than the one we would conjure up with proofs in the philosophy classroom. We are bidden to explore what tomorrow would look like, will look like, under this God's care.

A word about trust*

As for trust, the topic of this book, we need some preliminary words. "Basic trust," contended psychologist Erik Erikson, was the need on which other aspects of life are based. Children are not born independent, though they may cry as if they were; they are dependent on parents and others who bid them to trust them. When parents are neglectful or abusive, the child is rendered insecure, is shattered. When people shake hands over a deal, their subsequent

* Editor's note: Twenty years ago, Martin Marty wrote an Introduction to a volume called *The Place of Trust* (San Francisco: Harper and Row, 1983) now out of print. The material that follows in this section draws on material in the earlier introduction but has been reworked and updated for this volume.

action shows whether they were trustworthy or not. Marrying couples make pledges and vows, which are astonishingly precarious bids for trust, since they invited the other to count on them in sickness and in health, for better and for worse, knowing that if they make it to the end, one will close the eyes of the other.

We take human precautions to enhance trust. There are Trust Banks and Trust Funds, Trusts and Trustees. Usually we depend upon signatures, bonds, legal documents, safe deposit boxes, to back up the commitment to trust. There are no such documents or locks on human interaction, and when trust breaks down in that zone, mental health can disappear in devastation.

Philosopher Gabriel Marcel influenced my thinking on the nature of trust, and may well help you develop yours. For him, trust, whether in another person or, in this case, in God, connects with belief. "To believe in someone," means "to place confidence in him, is to say, 'I am sure that you will not betray my hope, that you will respond to it, that you will fulfill it.'" Luther anticipates this when he so often defines faith not as a "belief that" doctrines are true, though that also works. More often, faith means "belief in," in this case belief in God as Creator, Jesus as Savior, and the Holy Spirit who calls us to faith and communion.

Read the history of doctrinal controversy in the past or pay attention to it today, since it divides virtually every Christian communion, and you are likely to hear plenty of defenses of "belief that" by people that will not strike you as whole, balanced, profound, or possessing mental health. It is important not to overdo the picture of doctrinal zealots as fanatics, but to note how in defense of "belief that" it is especially easy to live a disguised life of being curved in upon one's self. You can look and act like God's protector, the defender of divine truth, and still be a nitpicker standing for what you have come to put together as the Absolute Truth package.

Longshoreman philosopher Eric Hoffer in *The True Believer* observed that some defenders of their version of "belief that" are moved less by love of truth than by mutual suspicion. Those of us who enjoy life in churches that are marked by common confessions of faith have to be reminded that they at their best are calls to "belief in." They tell others, not "this is what you must believe," but "this is who and what we are." Yes, we hope you will see why confessions and doctrines serve as setters of boundaries, but for us to say "you must" is an appeal to coercion and not freedom.

"Belief in" a God who liberates, on the other hand, also liberates believers from having to be always and only protective, pecksniffy, ready to wrap knuckles or inspire heresy trials. "Belief in" lets God be God, turns over to God some aspects of care for God's truth as humans grasp it. When it is expressed and demonstrated, it can help a community of Christians grow in trust.

Erik Erikson and the psychologists have marked the development of trust through passages of life. We can all observe this being antic- ipated in the Gospel records of Jesus, the friend of children. Jesus puts the child forward as an example, a sign of someone who shows what trust is when she puts her hand in the hand of a guarding par- ent. But parents can betray and do fail children as they grow, so the adolescent and young adult have to find new locales for trust.

When someone is aged and the lights are dimming and the fires get banked until only embers show, she or he can draw upon the resources of trust enjoyed through the trials and triumphs of life. Such people certainly carry on conversation with God, sometimes in ago- nized and sometimes in grateful form. God, I thank you that in times of temptation and my lapses you did not withdraw your love. God, I wonder where you were in the misfortune that befell our house and loved ones. God, you asked me to put my trust in you, and sometimes I had a rough time sustaining my role in placing trust.

What near-death experiences, expounded, often tell us—just as the witness of families and chaplains and pastors report—is that those who are weakened and who die in faith are those in whom trust is most vivid. Nothing shall separate, nothing does separate the trusting "believer in" from the God who invites trust. But getting from child-like trust to end-of-life commendation of one's self to God, is a demanding pilgrimage through life. It needs constant attention. Each new occasion calls forth a new expression of trust, especially when there do not seem many natural reasons to be trusting.

In medieval dramas there was often a character called Soul, someone like the Pilgrim in *Pilgrim's Progress*. We know what happens when Faust sells his "soul" to Mephistopheles. In the present book you and I are "Soul." Soul is not a spooky presence, a ghost in a machine, a pilot on the ship of life. Soul is our whole being, but especially our being when we are in conversation with God. Soul, on pilgrimage through life, needs charts for sea passages and maps for land trips. This book uses one provided by Martin Luther, to whom we have already referred.

Hitching a ride with Luther through the Sermon on the Mount

An aside: you do not have to be Lutheran to track Luther as he responds to the Sermon on the Mount. Many Lutherans, I among them, often explore "the world in front of the text" with figures like St. Francis or St. Bernard, or modern non-Catholics who are not identified with Luther in any direct churchly sense. He needs a bit of introduction here, perhaps for those of Lutheran persuasion and communion as much as for others. He often gets portrayed as the brash defender of the faith in the sense of "belief that," the stormy and self-assured reformer of the church in the 16th century.

If he was all that, he was not only that. Here he comes across as someone who mixed his struggle for faith with bold assertions of "belief in" God where his experience after dealing with texts like these was vivid. While he had his inner self with which to contend, he kept learning, life-long, that the structures and authority of church life could be instruments of God. But they dared not be the objects of trust themselves. In fact, he found good reasons to mistrust them. And when churches of evangelical character within his range replaced the

Roman Catholic churches and their hierarchy, he did not find them to be finished products any more than a text could be. The church always had to be reformed. It was also "at the same time" justified and sinful. It was, he said, a "becoming," not a "being," (in German, a *Werden* and not a *Sein*). Which meant one had to carry on conversation with texts in order to see it purified, fresh, and ready for mission.

For Luther everything finally came down to the character of God, a God who created, also a God of justice and judgment as well as a God of mercy and steadfast love. Such a God bid for trust. And in few places did he find more succinct bidding than in the Sermon on the Mount. Believers who never heard of Luther or other commentators on the Gospel texts, through the ages have been astounded and cheered at once when they read or heard the passages about trust in the Gospel of Matthew. When they add the comment of Luther, they deal not with Jesus as the disciples remembered him or with the forms of Gospel expression, but one more set of witnesses that can help them grasp interpretations in what we call theology.

Mention theology and you can scare people away. Yes, Luther used many classic words that end in "ation," such as justification, expiation, sanctification, propitiation (rarely), and the like. But what becomes clear at once here is his preference for short words, pithy expressions, epigraphs, artistic reaches. Who are the theologians in his commentary? None other than the singing birds, agents of God's care for creation doing what every small child could already understand, and what some jaded adults have forgotten.

Most people who know anything about the Gospels knows something from the Sermon on the Mount, and whoever knows the Sermon will recognize the sections I have chosen for Soul on pilgrimage. No doubt all believers know the Lord's Prayer and millions have memorized the Beatitudes and the cherished "be not anxious" pages. Because they are familiar, we may have to work harder to let them work on us than if they were startlingly new.

Instead of taking them head on, as we are commended to do in regular Bible reading, we will figuratively hitchhike with commentator Luther on our way. Sometimes I hear the words of the gospel read in church and, though the pages from which we read are old and the original texts are older, they strike the ears as impressively fresh and challenging. And when I read the words of Martin Luther, preached and then written in 16th century Saxony, they take for granted a world that seems farther away from our daily experience than does first century Palestine, made familiar through countless tellings. There is no use pretending that Luther's external environment matches ours. What of his inner experience?

Here not everything makes for an easy match either. It is well known that he was a troubled, guilty soul who took refuge in a monastery and who spoke regularly about his anxieties and temptations. He was a genius at self-reflection and, to some psychologists, a casebook instance of a person with a problem. Theologically, God was impinging vividly on his world. But the God who hovered, observed, sneaked up on, and kept accounts of the sinner Martin was a righteous judge. Luther took a long course of reflection, examination, searching, and study before the God who accounted him righteous while he was still a sinner—thanks to grace in Christ, faith in Christ—was most real to him.

Today, most of the time, most of us are not so impinged upon. If anything, God is not too near us but too remote, absent, eclipsed, silent, hard to recognize and harder to count on. Yet in remarkable ways Luther's experience and witness do translate to the world moderns inhabit, and the problems he addresses and the solutions he brings, you will find, have counterparts in the experience of most of us.

A publisher could be tempted to tempt me to plunder the 110 German volumes or the 55 English translations of much of them, in order to provide a garland of quotations. Luther's words are ripe for such plucking, since he is given to pithy expression (to balance his hour-long sermons, which are anything but pithy). Rather than follow that course, I have decided to select three longer passages, eliminating some extraneous material with some periods (. . .) along the way. These longer passages allow the voice of Luther to dominate, and he is not thus subjected to the picker of juicy quotations. I have been asked to break in between many of these longer passages to invite and instigate, perhaps to model, the wrestling with texts that we are here calling conversation.

When commending "the world behind" or "the world of" someone like Martin Luther to modern audiences, one could wish that everything he said was nice, polished, discreet, and empathic. It was not, for this at-the-same-time-justified-and-sinful being was flawed. He could use rough language—watch out for "bellies" and "bags of worms" and other crudities or, at least, realistic expressions. He could be as rude as he was crude at one moment and then disarmingly gentle at another. Yet historians of biblical interpretation list him as one of the few great "diviners" of Scripture. One of them explains this choice of term by reference to water witches, who used "divining rods." Believe them or not, they used a forked stick to walk along looking for water until something as if magnetic pulled the end to the ground, under which waters were supposed to be.

Whether or not there is anything to water witching, the picture of divining works well here. There have to have been even in his day more meticulous and accurate scholarly commentators. But he found where the waters streamed under the ground beneath us, and helped bring them forth, to refresh.

Note that not everything in the texts translated by my teacher and friend Jaroslav Pelikan was exactly the formulation of Luther. Don't picture him in front of a word processor or even long sheets of paper on which to scribble, though he did plenty of scribbling. These texts were sermons or classroom lectures, taken down by students in various shorthand styles, transcribed, and published. We know of instances where published versions show the influence of some of the note takers about whom we know something. But what we are after here depends not upon every iota of a text but of its gist, its drift. And you will "get the drift."

His drift reflects a world far from that of modern feminists, liberationists, political critics, capitalists, or those given to churchly niceties in an agricultural, village-centered, late-medieval, almost still feudal world. He assumes hierarchies that we would resist today. What surprises is how often beyond his captivity to his time is his ability also to transcend it, to speak to our own, to help us be more free of captivity to the fads and fashions, worries and concerns, dreams and visions of our world—one which is likely to be "dated" much more quickly and to more limiting effect than his world.

I hope that you carry from this book, then, not a new sense of Luther scholarship or Gospel analysis, but a sense of the presence of the one who is the Inviter to whom we say, "I am sure you will not betray my hope, that you will respond to it, that you will fulfill it." And follow that with the word in Matthew 6:9: "Pray, then, like this" . . . In trust.

For reflection

1. As you begin this "conversation" with Luther and the text of Matthew's Gospel, consider what place trust plays in your life. Do you consider yourself a trusting "Soul"? What, if anything, do you find most challenging about trusting, about not giving way to anxiety and worry?

2. What is both freeing and frustrating about Luther's teaching that we are *simul justus et peccator*?

3. Considering the extent to which we human beings are "curved in" upon ourselves, how might trust help "straighten" us out, help us see beyond ourselves?

4. Before you read further in this book, what question(s) do you have?

1

A Lesson from the Birds and the Flowers!

So, let the conversation begin. Note the presence of at least four voices—Jesus via the Gospel writer, Martin Luther, Martin Marty, and you, the reader (see "For Reflection"). The hope is that these voices—and others that join you—will enter into true dialog, a seamless conversation that cannot be fully captured on the printed page.

Therefore, I tell you, do not be anxious about your life, what you shall eat or what you shall drink, nor about your body, what you shall put on. Is not life more than food, and the body more than clothing? (6:25)

Luther: Listen . . . to what serving Mammon (the god of possession) means. It means being concerned about our life and our body, about what we should eat and drink and put on. It means thinking only about this life, about how to get rich here and how to accumulate and increase our money and property, as though we were going to stay here forever. The sinful worship of Mammon does not consist in eating and drinking and wearing clothes, nor in looking for a way to make a living and working at it; for the needs of this life and of the body make food and clothing a requirement. But the sin consists in being concerned about it and making it the reliance and confidence of your heart. Concern does not stick to clothing or to food, but directly to the heart, which cannot let a thing go and has to hang on to it. As the saying goes, "Property makes a person bold." Thus "being concerned" means clinging to it with your heart. I am not concerned about anything that my heart does not think about, but I must have a heart for anything about which I am concerned.

You must not tighten this text too much, however, as if it prohibited any kind of concern at all. Every office and station involves taking on certain concerns, especially being in charge of other people. As St. Paul says about spiritual offices in Christendom (Rom. 12:8): "He who rules, let him be careful." In this sense the head of a household has to be concerned about whether his children are being brought up properly; . . . if he neglects this, he does wrong . . . .

Christ is not talking here about this sort of concern. This is an official concern, which must be sharply distinguished from greed. It is not concerned for its own sake but for the neighbor's sake; it does not seek its own interests (1 Cor. 13:5), but even neglects them and forgets them in order to serve somebody else. Therefore it may be called a concern of love, something divine and Christian, not a concern devoted to its own advantage or to Mammon, militating against faith and love, and even interfering with the official concern. The man whose money is dear to him and who is on the lookout for his own advantage will not have much regard for his neighbor or for the office that involves his neighbor . . . .

Christ has forbidden this greedy concern and worship of Mammon as an idolatry that makes men enemies of God. Now He goes on with many statements, examples, and illustrations, intended to make greed so repulsive to us and to give it such an odious appearance that we will feel like spitting on it. First of all He says: "Is not life more than food? That is, you can and you must entrust your life, your body, and your soul to God. It does not lie within your power to preserve this for a single hour. What fools you are, then, if you do not entrust the needs of your body to Him, too, for Him to provide you with food and drink! It would be the greatest foolishness imaginable to be scrupulously concerned about getting food and drink but to be unconcerned about getting body and life or preserving them for an hour. That would be like being concerned about the beautiful decoration of your house hut not knowing who was going to live there, or being concerned in the kitchen about the preparation of a big, expensive meal but not having anybody to eat it." That is how we behave in our greed: we are concerned about the little things, and we never think of the big things. Such concern is really unnecessary and superfluous, in fact, foolish. Even though we were to be deeply concerned about our body and its life, this would not accomplish a thing, since it does not lie within our power even for a moment, any more than grain growing in a field where we did not do the planting, or silver in a mine where we did not put it . . . .

. . . Yet we go along in our blindness, although it is obvious that we should not be concerned about our body and life. Even if we were concerned, that in itself would have to make us become Christians and think: "You see, not even for a moment do I have my life in my own hands. Now, since I have to entrust my body and life to God, why should I have any doubts and concerns about my belly and about how it is to be fed for a day or two?" It is like having a rich father who would be willing to give me a thousand guldens, and then not trusting him to give me a groschen when I need it.

Marty: Today . . . the key word is *concern*, as in being concerned, and in learning about what to be concerned.

The concern has to be with what we possess and then with what possesses us. Most of us live in cultures where possession of what we need in life, and more, is readily available. Commentators regularly report that people in our lower middle class and upper lower class possess or can possess food and clothes, shelter and goods, on a level that only a small percentage of the world's citizens can take for granted. The availability of possessions makes it easy to assume that they are simply there, ours for the taking.

If that is as far as things went, there would be no problem for the words of the Gospel to address or to draw forth comment. The problem comes in, says Luther, when a god of possession comes on the scene, a god called Mammon. You will not find this god in temples or on icons, unless banks and dollar bills count. But banks and bills by themselves again are not the problem. Mammon takes over when possessions rule us. They do this—here comes that key word—when "concern" rears up.

Concern leads to thinking, but a peculiar kind of thinking: obsession with getting more, increasing, forgetting eternity and the nearness of a date when possessions will no longer be ours, will no longer be. Luther is nothing if not practical minded: he picks up from the Gospel what common sense tells him: that a provident God provided material means to meet material ends. We do, after all, or before all, have to be fed and clothed and sheltered. Arranging life to have access to food and clothing and shelter and—if you know Luther and his enjoyment of life—the good things of life is not the problem. The problem is: concern.

When concern is too central, it warps thinking and leads the thinker and possessor to relocate things and make them occupy the place in the heart that ought to remain empty of care and full of God. Up pops the object of concern as the object of Luther's concern: when the object is one's own need to be in control, to manage, to have tomorrow taken care of, there is no room for carefreeness and freedom in general. Almost humorously Luther uses the image of stickers and sticky things: it would not be a problem if concern stuck to objects we own or might own. It is a problem that they stick so well to the heart, which gets cluttered and then possessive and protective.

A proverb of the day, "Property makes a person bold," speaks to our day. Without letting the observers swell in pride for observing it: many of the CEOs and managers, the investors and counselors, acquire enough that some of them are emboldened. We made it; why can't everybody? We made it our way; if others can't find a way, let them suffer. We possess, which is a sign that we have a right to possession. I am going to get off that track quickly, since it is misleading the pilgrim to look at the problems of others, while here we are to focus on universal temptations. A very poor person who owns a cane or a tent or a cup may have to be preoccupied with hanging on to it, until that property makes her bold as much as stocks can do it to the wealthy. Let go of what sticks is the message.

I never thought of the concept of "tightening the text" until I read it here, and it is a fine one. Tighteners serve their purpose when a screw is loose or a load is ready to fall off a truck. But you can over-tighten belts and tourniquets, assignments and punishments, and, yes, texts. You can pinch them and squeeze them—it's called "literalism" until all the life and breath goes out of them. So we read: be careful, not all concern is bad.

Here is one of those places where archaic terms from a previous century can inform our own doings. Luther speaks of the fact that we all occupy "offices," which does not mean nooks, crannies, cubicles, or impressive executive furnished rooms. It refers to the "offices" we hold and we are, which is his way of speaking of our calling. Everyone has a calling. If the word applied most easily to professionals in the clergy, law, or medicine or to role-players in the military or corporate life, it applies equally to homemakers, senior citizens who have energy and wit to do little more than cheer those nearby or pray for all, to children in school, and those who teach them.

The cleric had better have the right kind of concern for the parishioner, the lawyer for the client, the physician or nurse for the patient, the leader for those in her command, the care-giver for homes and children. "Christ is not talking about this sort of concern" is the brisk and abrupt terminating word on the subject. Such concern is for others, not a sign of greed and the bad god Mammon. Call it "a concern of love, something divine and Christian," something that mattered in the century of Jesus, the 16th century, and the 21st alike. The ones who have the right kind of concern have a right to have concern for their own bodies. "Doing without," for the sake of others, does nothing good if it leads to bad health, stress, and distraction.

Suddenly the word "idolatry" comes into view: greedy concern is idolatry, and those who practice it are not neutrals. They are enemies of God. Luther can get a bit gross, when he finds Jesus quoted as making greed repulsive, odious, meriting our spit. Always, the object has to be not objects but the generous heart and the view and service of the other. Otherwise? Fools! Foolish! Decorate a house and not know who will live there? Prepare a banquet and have no one to serve? Here is a psychological insight: such preoccupations based on greed force us to look up close and lose the distance, to focus on the minuscule and petty cares and miss concerns that are worthy objects of the loving heart.

Martin Luther and John Calvin notably reminded people in their time that the heart does not allow for vacancy: one has either God or idol in it, and if the idol is not recognizable, it is probably more dangerous in its disguise. The heart, when full, is something that goes before us, that we can throw ahead of us, and then the rest of us has to catch up, to stay alive and productive. The heart filled with greed over possessions is too heavy to project.

To this point, the text before us can sound crabby, scolding, and condescending. Anyone who speaks about fools and foolishness can be read as proud and censorious more than wise. But the brash language here serves as an alarm, sounds like a blown whistle: listen, it seems to be saying. More reassuring words are ahead. They are.

Look at the birds of the air: they neither sow nor reap nor gather into barns, and yet your heavenly Father feeds them. Are you not of more value than they? And which of you by being anxious can add one cubit to his stature? (6:26-27)

Luther: You see, He is making the birds our schoolmasters and teachers. It is a great and abiding disgrace to us that in the Gospel a helpless sparrow should become a theologian and a preacher to the wisest of men, and daily should emphasize this to our eyes and ears, as if he were saying to us: "Look, you miserable man! You have house and home, money and property. Every year you have a field full of grain and other plants of all sorts, more than you ever need. Yet you cannot find peace, and you are always worried about starving. If you do not know that you have supplies and cannot see them before your very eyes, you cannot trust God to give you food for one day. Though we are innumerable, none of us spends his living days worrying. Still God feeds us every day." In other words, we have as many teachers and preachers as there are little birds in the air. Their living example is an embarrassment to us. Whenever we hear a bird singing toward heaven and proclaiming God's praises and our disgrace, we should feel ashamed and not even dare to lift up our eyes. But we are as hard as stone, and we pay no attention even though we hear the great multitude preaching and singing every day.

Look at what else the dear little birds do. Their life is completely unconcerned, and they wait for their food solely from the hands of God. Sometimes people cage them up to hear them sing. Then they get food in abundance, and they ought to think: "Now I have plenty. I do not have to be concerned about where my food is coming from. Now I have a rich master, and my barns are full." But they do not do this. When they are free in the air, they are happier and fatter. Their singing of Lauds and of Matins to their Lord early in the morning before they eat is more excellent and more pleasant. Yet none of them knows of a single grain laid away in store. They sing a lovely, long Benedicite and leave their cares to our Lord God, even when they have young that have to be fed. Whenever you listen to a nightingale, therefore, you are listening to an excellent preacher. He exhorts you with this Gospel, not with mere simple words but with a living deed and an example. He sings all night and practically screams his lungs out. He is happier in the woods than cooped up in a cage, where he has to be taken care of constantly and where he rarely gets along very well or even stays alive. It is as if he were saying: "I prefer to be in the Lord's. kitchen. He has made heaven and earth, and He Himself is the cook and the host. Every day He feeds and nourishes innumerable little birds out of His hand. For He does not have merely a bag full of grain, but heaven and earth."

Now Christ says: "Every day you see before your very eyes how the heavenly Father feeds the little birds in the field, without any concern on their part. Can you not trust Him to feed you as well, since He is your Father and calls you His children? Shall He not be concerned about you, whom He has made His children and to whom He gives His Word and all creatures, more than about the little birds, which are not His children but your servants? And yet He thinks enough of them to feed them every day, as if they were the only thing He is concerned about. And He enjoys it when they fly around and sing without a care in the world, as if they were saying: 'I sing and frolic, and yet I do not know of a single grain that I am to eat. My bread is not baked yet, and my grain is not planted yet. But I have a rich Master who takes care of me while I am singing or sleeping. He can give me more than all my worries and the worries of all people could ever accomplish.'" Now, since the birds have learned so well the art of trusting Him and of casting their cares from themselves upon God, we who are His children should do so even more. Thus this is an excellent illustration that puts us all to shame. We, who are rational people and who have the Scriptures in addition, do not have enough wisdom to imitate the birds. When we listen to the little birds singing every day, we are listening to our own embarrassment before God and the people. But after his fall from the word and the commandment of God, man became crazy and foolish; and there is no creature alive which is not wiser than he. A little finch, which can neither speak nor read, is his theologian and master in the Scriptures, even though he has the whole Bible and his reason to help him . . . .

Marty: After a scene set among the money-changers, the next one is in the classroom. The class comes to order. The teacher walks in. Not in Luther's world. The teachers fly in. He lived in a world of bishops and princes, doctors of Scripture and doctors of theology. One would expect him to ask us to listen to them, phrasing interpretations of the way of God in stentorian tones that issued from old-time pulpits. Instead we are supposed to listen to chirping and singing from the birds, "our schoolmasters and teachers." Sparrows, yet, who do not even have a Bachelor of Arts in the aviary.

Their chirping is their diagnoses: "Look," miserable people. Take a walk at five a.m. and you are likely to hear the curriculum unfold. Literally, say the birds, you have possessions that you think will make you secure, but are not. We have no possessions but do not worry about insecurity. Now we go back to what we read before: there are proper concerns. It is not necessarily against the ways of God to have Social Security, insurance, 401Ks, pensions; they belong to our "office," and can be seen as responses by good stewards to God as Creator. Preoccupied with them, however, we are not likely to take that early morning walk, to enjoy nature, to hear the lessons that Mr. Sparrow, B.A., or Ms. Nightingale, M.Mus., are singing, which means teaching.

Flying free or caged, they do not evidence concern or worry. Luther runs the birds and us, their listeners, through the liturgy and the hours: Lauds, Matins, Benedicite—his birds even sing in Latin—and all this to alert us to the fact that they are gospel preachers. We hear, perhaps too often, some words perhaps from St. Francis: "Preach the gospel; use words if necessary." The birds are doing it without words, thanks to the example of words in the Sermon on the Mount. The picture Luther presents is rather romantic. The world of birds is also a precarious, cruel world. There are predators that swoop from higher or sneak up from below them. There can be famine, and no seed to eat. They can be buffeted in the weather. Reflecting on that note of realism is valid, so far as it goes. But by now we have seen that it is likely to go into concern for possession, the god of Security now taking the place of Mammon in the heart.

The interest here is in the "how much more" comparison. Those anonymous birds get cared for. How much more valuable are you, with your name given with baptism, your identity and personality, your vocation and your mission. God would have priorities mixed up if God could take care of sparrows and be careless about you, about us. How do we know what we read here: that God "thinks enough" about birds, "enjoys" them as they flit and sing. If the birds are care-free, "how much more" ought the children of God move about without care. They do their singing by instinct, and we do not do ours though reason gives reasons to.

Again, the intrusive words come along: we rational beings are "crazy," "foolish," "embarrassed," while the birds as theologians know, or at least do, better. In Luther's world, it is not that we have got to do better; if we listen to them we are empowered and informed and we get to do better, namely, be carefree.

And why are you anxious about clothing? Consider the lilies of the field, how they grow; they neither toil nor spin. Yet I tell you, even Solomon in all his glory was not arrayed like one of these. But if God so clothes the grass of the field, which today is alive and tomorrow is thrown into the oven, will he not much more clothe you, O men of little faith? (6:28-30)

Luther: Here you have another example and analogy; according to it, the little flowers in the field, which cattle trample and eat, are to become our theologians and masters and to embarrass us still further. Just look at them grow, all adorned with lovely colors! Yet not one of them is anxious or worried about how it should grow or what color it should have, but it leaves these anxieties to God. And without any care or effort on its part God dresses it up in such lovely and beautiful colors that, as Christ says, King Solomon in all his glory was not so beautiful as one of these—indeed, no empress with all her ladies-in-waiting, with all her gold, pearls, and jewels. No king He could name was so rich or so glorious or so beautifully adorned as was Solomon. But with all his magnificent pomp and splendor, the king is nothing when compared with a rose or a pink or a violet in the field. In this way our Lord God can adorn anyone whom He chooses to adorn. That is really an adornment, a color that no man can make or match, an adornment that no one could or would surpass. Though they were to be covered with pure gold and satin, they would still say: "I prefer the adornment of my Master up there in heaven, who adorns the little birds, to that of all the tailors and embroiderers on earth."

Now, since He dresses and adorns so many flowers with such a variety of colors, and each has its own coat, more splendid than all the adornment in the world, why is it that we cannot have faith that He will dress us as well? What are the flowers and the grass in the field when compared with us? And what were they created for except to stand there for a day or two, to let themselves be looked at, and then to wither and turn into hay? Or as Christ says, they are "thrown into the oven" to be burned and to heat the oven. Yet our Lord God regards these tiny and transient things so highly that He lavishes His gifts upon them and adorns them more beautifully than any earthly king or other human being. Yet they do not need this adornment; indeed, it is wasted upon them, since, with the flower, it soon perishes. But we are His highest creatures, for whose sakes He made all things and to whom He gives everything. We matter so much to Him that this life is not to be the end of us, but after this life He intends to give us eternal life. Now, should we not trust Him to clothe us as He clothes the flowers of the field with so many colors and the birds of the air with their lovely feathers? He is speaking satirically, in order to describe how abominable our unbelief is and to make it look as ridiculous as possible. But it is the devil himself and the disastrous fall we committed that make it necessary for us to watch a whole world filled with birds and flowers opposed to us, denouncing our unbelief by their own example and appearance, and acting as our most sublime theologians. They sing and preach to us and smile at us so lovingly, just to have us believe. And yet we go right on letting them preach and sing, while we remain as greedy and selfish as ever. But to our eternal shame and disgrace each individual flower is a witness against us to condemn our unbelief before God and all the creatures until the Last Day. . . .

Marty: Not to belabor the point, or, belaboring the point, Luther does another round of taunting and chiding in efforts to guide us to better perceptions. What the Sermon on the Mount said about birds it now says about flowers, to make the same point, one on which Luther, in no hurry, concentrates. As with the birds, so with the flowers. By analogy, by example, they, too, teach. Some of the same images come up: the flowers are also theologians. Theology (*theos* + *logos*, word about God) in my book is the interpretation of the life of a people in the light of God as reference. The people now are those who trample, walk over or past, sniff or ignore wild flowers, and who need their existence to serve as interpreters of God's ways.

Think of Solomon. You have heard of the Queen of Sheba and her visit to him. Do you know this detail? See 1 Kings 10. When she heard of the fame of King Solomon, ("fame due to the name of the Lord," the writer took pains to say), she came to test him. She came to Jerusalem "with a very great retinue, with camels bearing spices, and very much gold, and precious stones." Later, after her testing and display of her wares and wisdom—she was what the young today would call "awesome"—Solomon laid it on. She saw "the house he had built, the food of his table, . . . the attendance of his servants, their clothing, his valets, and his burnt offerings that he offered at the house of the Lord, there was no more spirit in her." The awesome one was awed.

The Sermon on the Mount as interpreted by Luther would take us to such a scene and say to Queen and King, "You have not seen anything yet. Let us take you for a walk in the meadows, where the wild flowers outclass you both." On trips to Europe, we pass the gardens around the Louvre, the Prado, the Uffizi, the Rijksmuseum, and the other major galleries, and walk in to see the greatest art yet from the hand of humans. None of it surpasses the flowers in the cultivated garden or the wild flowers at the edge of the cities. And they are neither products of the hand of humans or cultivation of any sort. For Luther, God becomes humorist and satirist, "to describe how abominable our unbelief is and to make it look as ridiculous as possible." Point well taken.

Therefore do not be anxious, saying, "What shall we eat?" or, "What shall we drink?" or, "What shall we wear?" For the Gentiles seek all these things; and your heavenly Father knows that you need them all. (6:31-32)

Luther: Every day you see these illustrations before your very eyes, how God nourishes and feeds everything that lives and grows from the earth, clothes and adorns it so beautifully. Now let these illustrations persuade you to lay aside your anxiety and your unbelief and to remember that you are Christians and not heathen. Such anxiety and greed are appropriate to heathen, who do not know God or care about Him. It is really idolatry, as St. Paul says (Eph. 5:5; Col. 3:5) . . . .

"Since you are Christians," He says, "you dare not doubt that your Father is well aware of your need for all this, of the fact that you have a belly that needs food and drink and a body that needs clothing. If He did not know it, you would have reason to be concerned and anxious about how to provide for yourselves. But since He does know it, He will not forsake you. He is faithful and willing to take special care of you Christians, because, as has been said, He cares for the birds of the air as well. So forget your anxieties, since you cannot accomplish anything by them. It does not depend upon your anxiety but upon His knowledge and concern." If nothing grew in the field unless we were anxious about it, we would all have died in our cradles; and during the night, while we are lying asleep, nothing could grow. Indeed, even by worrying ourselves to death we could not make a single blade of grass grow in the field. We really ought to see and understand that God gives everything without any anxiety on our part, and yet we are such godless people that we refuse to give up our anxiety and our greed. Though it is up to Him to be concerned, as a father is concerned for his children, we refuse to leave it to Him.

Marty: People tell us not to worry, but we do. Often, when troubled, we turn and toss insomniacally through the night hours and wake unrefreshed. Sleep eludes us because we are not drifting in the present moment, but reflecting on past flaws—it's called "guilt"—or working on an agenda over which we have no control because it is tomorrow's, not here yet, and because we never will have complete control. Don't worry. Go to sleep.

It does not work that way, and in his autobiographical passages Luther confesses that he has not conquered concern for tomorrow. That is why he seems to be preaching so much to himself when he invokes a satirical God, and so emphatically to us. Get this right, he is saying, and the rest will follow. Reaching for more striking illustrations, repeating himself as he moves from the birds to the plants, all seems to be part of a strategy that will shake us loose from conventional ways of thinking and entertaining new ways.

At this point new characters enter the scene. In Matthew they are called "Gentiles," and Luther calls them "heathen" and us "godless." To ask for what they ask is too little, too self-preoccupying. Ask for more, be more, show more confidence, is the message. And here comes some more satire: not to be confident is to insult God's intelligence. That we have bellies is pretty obvious to us, especially if we are trying to shrink ours after having possessed and processed too much food. Is it not obvious to God, who made our bellies? If God did not know that we have them, and have need, we might worry, but since God knows, there is no reason for it. Everywhere the focus of Luther is on letting God be God, keeping God as the central character in our plots, knowing God as provident. Godlessness means not letting our knowledge that God is concerned lead us to leave worry to God.

For reflection

1. Reflect on the place Mammon, possessions, play in your life. What level of "concern" do you have for the "things" have or desire to have?

2. How do you respond to Jesus' words: "Do not be anxious about . . . what you will eat . . . and what you will put on"?

3. Many of us have an abundance of food, clothing, shelter, and things. When can such abundance become a "curse"?

4. What may we learn from the birds or the flowers of the field about anxiety and security, about priorities and peace?

5. The writers remind us that God knows us intimately, meaning God knows our needs better than we know them ourselves. Is this thought mostly comforting or mostly disturbing for you? Why?

6. What "word" (phrase, theme, or idea) has been especially meaningful for you in this chapter? What have you learned, or relearned?

2

Seek First the Kingdom

But seek first the kingdom of God and his righteousness, and all these things shall be yours as well. (6:33)

Luther: . . . It is important for the heart to realize what the kingdom of God is and what it grants. If we could be persuaded to give this some thought and if in our hearts we were to measure and weigh how much greater and more precious a treasure this is than Mammon or the kingdom of the world, that is, than everything on earth, then we would spit at Mammon. If you had the wealth and the might of the King of France and of the Turkish Emperor, what more would you have than a beggar at the door has with his crumbs? All that is really necessary is something to fill the belly every day. More than this no one can do, even if he has all the goods and all the glory in the world. The poorest beggar has as much of this as the mightiest emperor; and he may even get more enjoyment and benefit out of his crumbs than the emperor does out of a magnificent, royal repast. That is all there is to it, and no one gets any more out of it. It lasts only a brief and tiny while, and then we have to surrender it all. We cannot use it to extend our physical existence by a single hour when our hour comes. . . .

By these words, therefore, Christ would like to wake us up and say: "If you want to have the right sort of anxiety and concern about always having plenty, then seek for the treasure called 'the kingdom of God.' Do not be anxious about the temporal and perishable treasure which moth and rust consume . . . . You have a much different treasure in heaven, which I am pointing out to you. If you are anxious about that and seek it and if you keep in mind what you have in it, you will soon forget about the other one. This is the kind of treasure that will sustain you forever, and it cannot perish or be taken away.

Because the treasure you cling to is an enduring one, you will endure, too, even though you may not have a single (dollar) from the world."

What the kingdom of God is has often been stated. To put it most briefly, it does not mean outward things like eating and drinking (Rom. 14:17) nor other works that we can do. Rather, it means believing in Jesus Christ. In this kingdom He is the Head and the only King, in whom and through whom we have everything; whoever abides in it cannot be harmed by any sin, death, or misfortune, but has eternal life, joy, and salvation. Here he begins in this faith, but on the Last Day all will be revealed, and he will be eternally perfected in it.

Now, what does it mean to "seek" this kingdom? What is the method of reaching it, and what way or path leads to it? Here one points in one direction, another in another direction. This is what the pope teaches: "Run to Rome and get an indulgence, confess and do penance, read or hear Mass, put on a cowl, and discipline yourself with long services and a strict, ascetic life." We used to run in every direction we were told to run, like crazy and foolish people. We all wanted to seek the kingdom of God, but all we found was the kingdom of the devil. For there are many ways, but they are all departures from that one way of believing in Christ and practicing and applying the Gospel, to which faith clings. This involves growing and being strengthened at heart through preaching, listening, reading, singing, meditating, and every other possible way. And it involves blossoming out in fruits, to advance it and to lead many other people to it . . . . If you want to know (the kingdom) and find it, you must not seek for it on the basis of your own ideas. You must hear His Word, as the foundation and cornerstone, and see where He directs you and how He interprets it. Now, this is His Word about His kingdom (Mark 16:16): "He who believes and is baptized will be saved." The Word was not spun out of our own heads, nor did it grow out of any human heart. It fell from heaven and was manifested by the mouth of God, to give us certainty and to keep us from missing the right path. Now when both the preachers and the hearers proceed as they should in the diligent use of Word and Sacrament, when they consistently apply this in their lives to make it known among the people, and when they bring in the young people and teach them, then they are really seeking and promoting the kingdom of God and taking it seriously.

Now, what does He mean by adding "and His righteousness"? This kingdom has a righteousness of its own, but a righteousness different from that in the world, since it is a different kingdom. Thus it refers to the righteousness that comes from a faith that is busy and active in good works. It means that I take the Gospel seriously, that I listen to it or use it diligently, and that then I actually live in accordance with it instead of being an idle fellow or a hypocrite, who lets it come in through one ear and out through the other. The Kingdom proves its presence in deed and in power, as St. Paul says (1 Cor. 4:20): "The kingdom of God does not consist in talk but in power." That is what we call the Gospel with its fruits—doing good works, fulfilling your station or office diligently and faithfully, and undergoing all sorts of suffering for the Gospel. He uses "righteousness" here in a general sense for the whole life of a Christian in relation to God and man, including both the tree and its fruit, not in the sense that it is completely perfect. It is continually progressing, as He shows here by telling His disciples to keep on seeking it, since they have not yet obtained it (Phil. 3:12) or learned it or lived it perfectly. For our condition in the kingdom of Christ is half sin and half holiness. What there is in us that belongs to faith and to Christ is completely pure and perfect, since it is not our own but Christ's, who is ours through faith and who lives and works in us. But what is still our own is completely sinful. Yet under Christ and in Him it is concealed and blotted out through the forgiveness of sins; and daily it is put to death through the same grace of the Spirit, until we have died to this life altogether . . . .

. . . To (His) admonition He now adds a promise and a consolation, to keep us from thinking that since we have to suffer so much from a world that denies and begrudges us everything and since every hour we are expecting to have it all taken away from us, He wants to give us nothing at all on earth and to let us starve. We should know that here, too, we shall have what we require for the necessities of this life. That is why He says: "If you just seek the kingdom of God first, then all these things shall be yours as well." That is, you shall receive food and drink and clothing as a bonus, without any anxiety of your own. In fact, it will come by the very fact that you are not anxious about such things and that you risk everything for the sake of the kingdom of God, and in such a way that you will not know where it came from, as our experience teaches us every day. . . .

Marty: Today . . . "Kingdom" is the word that serves to organize this day. "Seek first the kingdom of God . . . . "

Countless definitions contend whenever anyone mentions "kingdom of God." In some hymns like Timothy Dwight's "I Love Your Kingdom, Lord," kingdom turns into "church." Dwight goes on to amplify that the kingdom is "the place of your abode."

Congregations sometimes call all their churchly activity "kingdom work." Such equating is credible, but not accurate. It has been said that the church is not the kingdom, but it presupposes the kingdom.

Mouth the word today, turn it over in your mind, and see what comes to mind. What is it that we "seek first" if we seek the kingdom of God. If I had to sort through all the definitions and choose one that most applies in contexts like this in Matthew 6 and in so much of the Gospels, it would distance itself from anything that sounds like a collection of buildings or an institution, both of which can be informed and driven with energy from the kingdom.

From corners of my brain, stored there since theological school fifty years ago and more but whose source I cannot now identify, was something like this: kingdom is the sovereign saving activity of God in Jesus Christ.

Take it apart.

"Sovereign" means that God rules. Others may and do serve under God, but no one serves above God. This sovereign, unlike so many earthly counterparts, is not tyrannous. Recognizing this non tyrannical sovereign gives perspective and proportion. Awed by the Sovereign, those who rise from having bowed or been struck will never again be dazzled by or subservient to those who are not sovereign, but only vice-regents at best and pretenders at worst.

"Saving" refers to the central theme of kingdom life. Earthly kingdoms belong to the "curved in upon themselves" school. They insist on being saved and served. They determine ranks of others and look out for their own good. Instead, the kingdom of God is saving, in that its agents speaking in the name of its Sovereign look not out for themselves but diagnose the petty rule that enslaves people on earth and liberates them. We rise today and go to bed tonight aware that we are situated where God's care is immediate. We are free of bonds; we are in the scope of what God wills and does.

"Activity" is the third key word in this definition. It serves again to remind us that kingdom is not a place, not a thing, but an agency, a center and sign and seal of action. Where God is present, where Jesus Christ is advancing the kingdom, where Matthew reproduces words about the kingdom and Luther comments on them, you can spot the kingdom anywhere but one place, in almost any form except the static. God is always actively present wherever creativity is going on. God is ardent and in motion when someone is being made just or experiencing salvation. God is present where the Spirit stirs, always actively.

That all this happens in Jesus Christ is obvious in Luther's accounting, for Jesus is the Word, and without the Word, "let there be," there will be no created universe. Without the Word "made flesh" in Jesus there will not be saving, since God concentrates the work of salvation, of rescue and imparting wholeness, in the human Jesus who is the exalted Lord. Without the Word the letters of the Bible would be lifeless, but now the Word comes in, and as the Holy Spirit.

Sovereign. Saving. Activity. In Jesus Christ. With that in mind we hear: "But seek first the kingdom of God and His righteousness."

That little word "but" has to work as a great lever, since it carries a heavy burden. It has to serve as a well-oiled axle in the middle of the sentence, since so much turns on it. We have just heard how natural it is for us to ask, in anxiety, about material things, to eat or wear. It is natural to concentrate on the visible, the palpable, the tangible, that which is up close, and quite natural to miss the motion of God toward the universe, toward believers, toward individual hearts. Be not anxious, BUT seek. . . .

When Luther sets out to define what the kingdom of God is and what it grants, he does not use abstract language such as "saving" and "activity." For him it is all full of pithy, concrete, vibrant touchables such as a "treasure." He is almost more concerned with what it is not, what it displaces or obscures: Mammon, the kingdom of the world, everything on earth, wealth, the might of rulers, magnificent royal repasts. All those "things" last only a "brief and tiny while," hardly more than a mini-second.

The kingdom of God is heavy, precious, lasting, satisfying, worthy of our preoccupation this day. Luther joins the company of those who write *memento mori* lines: remember that you must die. The wealth and might of French and Turkish rulers, much on his mind, did not do more for them than did the crumbs serve the beggar at the door. The beggar might appreciate the crumbs more than the rulers enjoy the prerogatives of their rule. "That is all there is to it," says Luther, reminding readers "you must die. We have to surrender it all." In Luther's time there reigned Henry VIII in England, who gorged at table and induced vomiting so he could gulp more. Luther posits the obvious, but here with the proclamation of the Sermon on the Mount that all of that is not worth the effort; none of it extends physical life at all.

Just as we were earlier told to have concern, but concern of the right kind, now we find it linked with anxiety, but anxiety of the right kind.

"The right sort of anxiety" focuses not on having enough but for that which goes beyond the perishable and the temporal. Now it becomes "treasure in heaven," now possessed but not realized. Focus on it liberates one from concern for the passing show and its baubles. The treasure of the kingdom endures, so you, if you cling to it—hold on, it's activity, and it moves—"you will endure, too," even if penniless.

Luther's definition concludes by reference to "believing in Jesus Christ" and thus "having everything." So far so good. But another definition awaits us. It has to do with the little word "seek" as in "seek first the kingdom of God." Luther can have gotten himself into trouble here, because "seeking" can often get its propulsion from anxiety and self-concern. Someone who lies back, lounging in expectation for the word of grace, does not strike the observer as someone in the activity of "seeking." To seek usually implies some concern about finding and anxiety about not finding.

So we need direction. But Luther pictures us seekers being confused not by lack of direction but by competition between the directions to which people point. One direction. Another direction. Plenty are available, but here, once more briskly and brashly it comes at us: "they are all departures from that one way of believing in Christ and practicing and applying the Gospel, to which faith clings." This seems in at least some extreme cases to run against the graceful notion of being searchers on a spiritual journey or faithful efforts at joining a seekers' church, since these routes may appeal to the compulsively anxious, those who take things in and remain curved in upon themselves.

Luther has a little assignment pad for seeking: growing, being strengthened, through "preaching, listening, reading, singing, meditating, and every other possible way." And then, blossoming. Before, we anticipated what has to come next for anyone who would follow Luther and his discipline. "You must not seek for the Kingdom on the basis of your own ideas." "Kingdom" is not a word that neatly matches all that goes with modern spirituality, finding the God that is your inner self. Only God's Word, belief, and Baptism point you to the true kingdom.

There must be easier ways to use spirituality to move into the kingdom of God. It would not be hard to think up a story of sovereign saving activity that did not center on an infant, a sufferer, someone betrayed who dies. Most any story that might come to mind would be more credible, more worthy of commendation. Go ahead and invent. Luther points to a roadblock. The story of being saved is too peculiar, too special, too idiosyncratic, to do all that it should. "The Word was not spun out of our own heads, nor did it grow out of any human heart. It fell from heaven . . . . " Luther's agenda was basic: preach and hear preaching; offer the Sacrament and receive it; bring in a new generation and teach it all to them.

The words in Luther's paragraphs here are in conflict with the notions of spirituality not centered in God as the Other whom we meet, who meets us. Word often goes out that we should undertake disciplines that will make us spiritual, and that's that. Be religious. George Santayana wrote that we do not speak language; we speak a language, if we want to be intelligible to anyone, especially if they speak the language. Yes, religions and spiritualities may have much in common—the pursuit of human dignity, the sacredness of the created order—but their saving power, he wrote, is in the surprising and idiosyncratic stories each of them tells. So it works here, too: do not just "seek" or "seek a kingdom" but seek a specified kingdom and God's righteousness.

"Righteousness" is the next word that causes Luther to draw up short, and that he then turns to get our attention. Seek the kingdom of God and God's righteousness. Luther dated his move into reform of the church from his discovery—if not for the whole church, at least for his hungry soul—that Paul connected "righteousness" and "faith" in a way different from what he, and before him Paul as well as many in our time, were taught. Righteousness had meant the character and expression of an all-seeing, scorekeeping, actively angry

God who could annihilate him. It was active, and Luther thought it was alien to the purposes and character of the God of mercy. He said he hated the God of such righteousness.

As nights passed with tossing in bed and days with study, Luther came to see that the righteousness that counted was passive, which meant God took it all in. It was God's proper work to regard God's frail people as declared just. This righteousness comes in the conversation with God, when we listen and use diligently the gospel that we now take seriously. It is a righteousness that animates humans to live in accordance with it. It is a kingdom less of words than of power. The gospel impels good works, living into one's vocation, and being ready for suffering for the gospel.

In this context Luther voices something similar to his formula that we are at the same time declared just and found to be sinners: "For our condition in the kingdom of Christ is half sin and half holiness." That phrasing has some merit, but Luther declares it more baldly and boldly when he says that the human is utterly made just and remains utterly the sinner. "Half and half" sounds more mild, but we know what he is getting at. This righteousness that goes with the kingdom is "continually progressing," since no one has attained it. Then he gets more extreme: what there is in us that belongs to faith and to Christ is completely "pure and perfect, since it is not our own but Christ's." And again, extremely, "what is still our own is completely sinful." Extreme meets extreme, yet there is progress. As mentioned in the Introduction, the kingdom of God is among us a *Werden*, a becoming, and not a *Sein*, namely, a being.

The sinner is "made perfect" by God's act of declaring her just, but is not perfect from the angle of human vision and acting. In an interview the 93-year-old clarinetist Artie Shaw reminisced about his mastery of his instrument, which he laid down fifty years ago. Why? Because people told him, and he knew he was as near being perfect at it as he could be. Then the interviewer asked him how he was now. "Well, not perfect. My knee is not perfect." And then he mused, "But then, even when I was perfect I wasn't perfect."

In God's eyes, the one declared just is perfect as Christ is perfect, but is not perfect as a human with the blight and error that goes with the mortal condition. Still, "half and half," or "completely and completely," as Luther voices it in a parallelism, righteous believers in action are not perfect when they are perfect. They seek the kingdom, where more awaits them.

Luther can never proceed too far in analyzing, scolding, or advising, without turning his attention and language to the counterpart. To Jesus' admonition, he "now adds a promise and a consolation." So commentator Luther turns pastoral and examines why. Here is the answer: we are not to think that since the world denies and begrudges us everything, and since any hour we can be taken away from everything God "wants to give us nothing at all on earth." Wrong. At the very least we have necessities. And drink and clothing come as a bonus. You cannot calculate, that by giving the appearance of seeking the kingdom, God will be fooled into awarding a bonus. Instead, without our pushing, striving, or anxiety, the bonus comes "by the very fact that you are not anxious about such things," and are ready to risk all for the kingdom. All this adds up to giving us reason to know where the bonus comes from. Luther thought that "our experience teaches us (that) every day." *Maybe* it does, says the eye of reason. It does, affirms the eye of faith.

Therefore do not be anxious about tomorrow, for tomorrow will be anxious for itself. Let the day's own trouble be sufficient for the day. (6:34)

Luther: "Let this be your concern," He says, "how to retain the kingdom of God. And get rid of the other concerns so completely that you are not even concerned about tomorrow. When tomorrow comes, it will bring its own concerns along." As we say, "Do not cross your bridges until you come to them." Our concern accomplishes nothing anyway, even though we are concerned for only one day at a time. Experience shows that two or three days often pass by faster than today. If God is kindly disposed to a man and gives him success, he can often accomplish more in one hour without care and anxiety than another man in four whole days with great care and anxiety. Whereas the one has dragged on with his anxiety and made it tedious for himself, the other has disposed of it in an hour. Thus no one can accomplish anything except when the hour comes that God gives as a free gift without our anxiety. It is vain for you to try to anticipate and with your concern to work out what you think are great schemes.

Our Lord God knows the art of secretly shortening and lengthening times and hours for us, to make one hour become two weeks for someone, and vice versa. Thus with long labor and sorrow one person accomplishes no more than another person with short and easy work. This is evident every day. There are many people who work steadily and hard but barely make ends meet, while there are others who have arranged and ordered their affairs so well that without any particular effort everything goes along smoothly, and they prosper. God works it all this way to keep us from supposing that our anxiety necessarily brings His blessing. But we refuse to wait for God to add these good things to us. Instead we insist on finding them for ourselves before God gives them. . . .

Now, since you see that it is pointless and that your anxiety is useless, why not give it up and think instead about how to get the kingdom of God? He wants to be generous to you, but not on account of your being concerned or even on account of your working. It is not such concern that gains and accomplishes anything, but rather the concern that is part of your office. The kingdom of God requires you to do what you are commanded to do, to preach and to promote the Word of God, to serve your neighbor according to your calling, and take whatever God gives you. The best possessions are not the ones that come from our planning, but the ones that come by chance and from His generosity. The things that we have acquired or planned to keep by being anxious will probably be the first to collapse and be ruined. . . It is a great gift of grace that God does not make it our concern how the grain is growing in the field, but gives it to us while we are lying asleep. Otherwise we would ruin it with our anxiety, and we would get nothing.

Therefore He says now: "Why be concerned about more than the present day and take on the troubles of two days? Be content with the trouble that the present day lays upon you. Tomorrow will bring you another one." He calls it a "trouble" or a plague laid upon us that we have to make a living in the sweat of our face (Gen. 3:19) and endure all sorts of other accidents, worries, misfortunes, and dangers every day. Daily in this life we must see and expect such trouble, when something is stolen from you or you suffer some other damage or when you get sick or when your servants do. Suffer such sorrow, anguish, and trouble, and receive it with joy. Be content with that, for it is enough for you to bear. Forget about your anxiety, which only increases and aggravates the trouble. From these examples you can see that God never used anyone's anxiety to make him rich; in fact, many people have the deepest kind of anxiety, and still they have nothing. What He does is this: when He sees someone fulfilling his office diligently and faithfully, being concerned to do so in a God-pleasing way, and leaving the concern over its success to God, He is generous in His gifts to such a person. It is written (Prov. 10:4): "The hand of the diligent makes rich." . . . He commands you to get an honest grip on your work, and then He will be present with His blessing and give you plenty. . . .

Marty: Here is a downer: we are not to be anxious about tomorrow, "for tomorrow will be anxious for itself." And then, "let the day's own trouble be sufficient for the day." Tomorrow means the future; the day means the present. There go our two favorite tenses. The past is all right for the delight of historians and the bittersweet happy melancholia of the nostalgic. But the problem is that it is past. "O God, Our Help in Ages Past," duly sung about deserves praise, but Soul asks, what has God done for us lately, what is God doing now, and what will God be doing through us in the promise of the kingdom?

Luther often resorts to proverbs, only some of which lapse into cliché, as does this one about tomorrow: "Do not cross your bridges until you come to them." This one is satisfying to the degree it implies that the bridge is crossable and that we will be able to cross it. It is unsatisfying at the same time because the hazards of the bridge presented tomorrow may be forbidding, murderous. Luther uses the moment to discuss the relativity of time as experienced. Tomorrow? God accomplishes more through the unanxious in one hour than in four whole days when another has care and anxiety. Each hour is God's free gift, and those relieved of anxiety use each most productively.

"Our Lord God knows the art,"—what a quaint way to speak of the maker of all arts—"of secretly shortening and lengthening times and hours for us, to make one hour become two weeks for someone, and vice versa." Luther knows something about *ennui* and something about spirited production, and what each experience does to the sense of motion and time. Instead of moralizing about the low achievers, he uses it to remind us that by relativizing the sense of time God keeps us from thinking that we produce God's blessing through our worry and anxiety. The message: wait, don't strive. This looks like psychological counsel worth listening to; it is theological counsel in any case, since it refers to the character of God and God's bearing toward us.

Joseph Sittler, a theologian who influenced so many of us, was once asked what was a Christian. He smiled and all but instantly snapped back: "A Christian is someone who accepts what God gives him or her in Christ." Maybe he was reflecting this passage from Luther. First come commands that go with the office each of us holds: preach, promote, serve, and then "take whatever God gives us," his recipe for relieving anxiety. What we plan for is not as satisfying as what comes by chance and through divine generosity. It's worth reflecting on that proposition on the basis of our several personal experiences; conversing with Luther, we may not all come out at the same point of agreement with it. But he follows the spirit of the Sermon on the Mount when he explains that the things we strive for are more likely to induce anxiety, and they "will probably be the first to collapse and be ruined." Let the grain grow while we sleep; it will grow as well as if we stay awake and worry.

Luther tries to soften the brunt of the word "troubles," but begins by doing a terrible job. Troubles that come in the day that is present include plague, sweat, accidents, worries, misfortunes, and dangers. The catalog goes on at such length one would just as soon not dwell on the details: something is stolen, we suffer damages, get sick. He will not gain many natural points by urging that we are to receive with joy "sorrow, anguish, and trouble," something he did not always do. But he is back on track reminding that anxiety only aggravates the trouble and, at best, does no good at all. Each does the best he or she can, carefreely in the appropriate office, and turns concern over success to God. That observation will not make it into any of the executive or middle manager success manuals, but is more likely to produce achievement than they do.

This has been an essay on getting rid and letting go. Some years ago a dear friend with a terminal illness wanted to liberate her children in advance of the grieving they would do after she died. And she wanted to liberate herself from the need to grasp and hold on to what she surely had to let go of when the troubles of today and the new troubles of tomorrow had passed. She had each grown child come home and lie next to her on the bed covers as they took inventory of what it is they could learn to do without. What about that ornate gold frame around Dad's picture? That could go; we never liked it anyhow. So that did not count. What about that picture of Dad? That was harder. They had to let it go. Please don't set this book down having seen it as a lesson in tossing Dad's picture into the wastebasket. The reference is to remind us that thought for the morrow does not serve well.

Take no thought for tomorrow. A personal word: when my first wife was terminally ill, I spent nine months in a combined study-bedroom with her, but at her bidding left at six each morning to return at noon, to keep up a teaching schedule. I would wake to bleakness and blackness of a sort those terminally ill or near such ill loved ones will recognize. A bit of therapy occurred twenty minutes later when I whipped onto the expressway and saw hundreds of autos already whizzing people to their day's "office." That meant rejoining the human race, just as the arrival of company meant for her.

Still, there was a profound nagging, even gnawing. The buzz of traffic and the day's doings only helped situate me in the present half way. Tomorrow still impinged. Then a good counselor asked my wife and me the same question: Is the pit-deep anxiety you feel "about" today? We would think hard. No. We had awakened to another day with its mix of troubles and brighter spots. We knew we had strength for today. We were concerned about some faceless, dateless, unknown tomorrow. Then the Sermon on the Mount type question: "Do you think that God will get you through every day but the one you most need God, most rely on God?" No.

After realizing that "no" we could move forward, knowing that the strength and courage promised and needed would be supplied on the day that counted, when it came. It was.

Now I still have to think about whether what comes by chance betters that than what comes from our planning. Throw in Luther's word after "chance," also "from His divine generosity" and it appears in a different light. If you have not found your definitive way of answering the question about planning versus chance, don't worry. Tomorrow it will still be there, to be treated afresh then.

Reflection questions

1. Based on what you have read in this chapter, how would you define God's "kingdom"? How might you, or do you, seek it?
2. Seeking implies action ("to seek usually implies some concern about finding and anxiety about not finding"). If seeking is not equated with "saving ourselves," since that is clearly God's work, what is the point of Jesus saying, "seek first the kingdom"?
3. One of the things we are called to seek is righteousness. What is "righteousness"? How will one know when he or she has found it?
4. How do you respond to the following: "Each hour is God's free gift, and those relieved of anxiety use each most productively"?
5. How can we reconcile the admonition to seek God's kingdom with the following comment: "What we plan for is not as satisfying as what comes by chance and through divine generosity."
6. What would you say is the most significant growth point or "learning" for you in this chapter?

3
Ask

Ask, and it will be given you; seek, and you will find; knock, and it will be opened to you. For every one who asks, receives, and he who seeks, finds, and to him who knocks it will be opened. Or what man of you, if his son asks him for a loaf, will give him a stone? Or if he asks for a fish, will give him a serpent? If you, then, who are evil, know how to give good gifts to your children, how much more will your Father who is in heaven give good things to those who ask him! (7:7-11)

Luther: . . . Christ, the Lord . . . adds an admonition to prayer. By this He intends to teach them that, second only to the office of preaching, prayer is the chief work of a Christian. . . . He also wants to indicate that because of all the temptations and hindrances we face, nothing is more necessary in Christendom than continual and unceasing prayer that God would give His grace and His Spirit to make the doctrine powerful and efficacious among us and among others. That is why, in the words we quoted from the prophet Zechariah (Zech. 12:10), God promised that He would pour out upon the Christians a Spirit of grace and of supplication. In these two items He summarizes all Christian existence.

Now, what He intends to say is this: "I have given you instructions about how you ought to live and what you ought to watch out for. In addition, it is necessary that you ask and that you have the confidence to go right on seeking and knocking without becoming lazy or lax in it. You will have need of asking, seeking, and knocking." Though doctrine and life may both have begun all right, we shall have to suffer from all sorts of transgressions and offenses that hinder us daily and keep us from progressing. We battle against these continually with all our might, but the strongest shield we have is prayer. If we do not use that, it is impossible for us to hold our own and to go on being Christians. We can plainly see now not only the sort of obstacles that oppose the Gospel every day, but also our own neglect of prayer and our attitude, as though this warning and admonition did not refer to us and we did not need prayer any more, now that the useless chattering and muttering of the rosaries and the other idolatrous prayers have stopped. All this is not a good sign, and it makes me afraid that some great misfortune which we could have prevented will overtake us.

Therefore every Christian should pay attention to this admonition. It is, in the first place, a commandment, as much as the previous statement, "Judge not" is a commandment. He should know that he is obliged to practice this Christian work. He should not be like that peasant who said: "I give grain to my minister, and he prays for me"; or like the people who think: "What is the use of my praying? If I do not pray, others do." We must not suppose that it is no concern of ours or that it is left up to our free choice. . . . In the second place, you have here the comforting promise and rich assurance that He attaches to prayer, to make it evident that He cares about it and to teach us to think about prayer as something dear and precious before God, because His admonition is so serious and His invitation so friendly, and He promises that we shall not ask in vain. Even if we had no other reason or attraction than this rich and friendly word, it should be enough to prompt us to pray. I shall not even talk about how dear His exhortation is or how sublime His command or how desperate our need.

Our own desperate need should be enough to make us pray. But in addition, as though that were not enough, He seeks to draw us to it by means of the beautiful analogy of every father's relation to his son. Though the son may be a good-for-nothing scamp, still he will not give him a serpent when he asks him for a fish. From that he draws these consoling words: "If you can do this, though you do not have a good nature or a single good trait in comparison with God, will not God, your heavenly Father, whose nature is completely good, give you good things if you ask Him for them?" This is the most sublime attraction by which anyone can be persuaded to pray, if we just looked at these words and took them to heart.

We have already spoken of the need that prompts Him to give this admonition and should prompt us to ask. Once you have the Word of God right and have made a good start in both doctrine and life, then inevitably temptation and opposition arise, not one kind but thousands of kinds. In the first place, there is our own flesh . . . It quickly becomes bored, inattentive, and indifferent to the Word of God and the good life. Thus we always have less of wisdom and of the Word of God, of faith and love and patience, than we should. This is the first enemy hanging around our neck so heavily every day that he keeps dragging us that way. Next comes the second enemy, the world. It begrudges us the dear Word and faith and refuses to put up with anything in us, no matter how weak we may be. It goes ahead and condemns us, it tries to take away what we have, and it gives us no peace. . . .

But getting ourselves to the point of praying causes us distress and anguish, and this requires the greatest skill. With our own concerns and thoughts we torture ourselves and stew over trying to pull this off our neck and to get rid of it. There is an evil and clever devil riding me and other people and frequently playing these tricks on me in my temptation or anxiety, whether it has to do with spiritual or with secular affairs. He immediately butts in and makes you start stewing over it. In this way he snatches us from our prayer and makes us so dizzy that we do not even think of praying. By the time you begin praying you have already tortured yourself half to death. He is well aware of what prayer achieves and can do. That is why he creates so many obstacles and disturbances, to keep you from getting around to it at all. Hence we ought to learn to take these words to heart. We should develop the habit, to fall on our knees immediately and to spread the need before God, on the basis of this admonition and promise. Then we would find help and would not have to torture ourselves with our own ideas about looking for help. This is a very precious medicine, one that certainly helps and never fails, if you will only use it. . . .

Why does Christ use so many words? He lists three items: "Ask, and it will be given you; seek, and you will find; knock, and it will be opened to you." One would have been enough. It is evident . . . that by this He intends to admonish us even more strongly to pray. He knows that we are timid and shy, that we feel unworthy and unfit to present our needs to God. We feel the needs, but we cannot express them. We think that God is so great and we are so tiny that we do not dare to pray. . . . That is why Christ wants to lure us away from such timid thoughts, to remove our doubts, and to have us go ahead confidently and boldly. Though I am unworthy, I am still His creature; and since He has made me worthy of being His creature, I am also worthy of receiving what He has promised and so generously offered to me. In other words, if I am unworthy, He and His promise are not unworthy. You can venture on this vigorously and trustfully, you can put it in His lap joyfully and confidently. But above all, be sure that you really believe in Christ and that you have a proper occupation, one that pleases God, so that you are not like the world, which does not care about its occupation but only about the vices and the villainy that it goes right on planning day and night. . . .

. . . For you have His Word, and He will have to say: "All right, then, you may have what you want." St. James speaks of this in his Epistle when he says (James 5:16): "The prayer of a righteous man has great power in its effects" if it is serious and persistent; and in support of this he cites the example from the Scriptures of the prophet Elijah (James 5:16, 17). By urging you not only to ask but also to knock, God intends to test you to see whether you can hold on tight, and to teach you that your prayer is not displeasing to Him or unheard, simply because His answer is delayed and you are permitted to go on seeking and knocking.

Marty: This time the word that draws attention is "ask." Some people find it important to say that Jesus in the Gospels speaks in and of absolutes. Some of his commands sound absolutist: "Be ye perfect (Matthew 6:48)." The Sermon on the Mount has many counsels that sound totalist in their demands. No escape. How to interpret that feature of his teaching—one that shows that God cannot be half-serious any more in commands than in promises—we leave for theologians on other days who deal with other parts of the text.

We have instead before us what sounds absolute and does not come accompanying a command. "For everyone who asks, receives, and he who seeks, finds, and to him who knocks it will be opened." That "everyone" sounds as shocking as the fact that the ask/receive, seek/find, knock/opened combinations are not preceded by words such as "often"— as in he "often receives," or "usually" as in "usually finds," or "regularly" as in "regularly be opened." No, there's a simply equal and opposite reaction to each of these actions. Tit for tat. Back and forth. Cause and effect. All unbroken.

The words of Jesus posed in the Sermon on the Mount often have a "can't duck" character that is disruptive enough of complacency. The one who hates has already killed (5:22). The one who has lusted has already committed adultery (5:28). The one who has coveted has already stolen. Comic W. C. Fields once said that he had been study- ing the Bible for fifteen years, "looking for a loophole." No loopholes in the Sermon on the Mount. For this moment, however, it is nat- ural to hope that there are no loopholes, no holes of any sort. Receiving, finding, and seeing something opened are such rich promises that we hope there will be no exceptions.

Despite the hopes, it does not always appear to be the case. Earlier in the Sermon on the Mount, in a passage about sparrows not quoted here, Jesus assures us that we should consider the birds and learn from them that none falls to the ground without the Father's knowledge. The uncomfortable feature of that, one we might like to slide over without noticing, is that they all do fall, with God's knowledge, but what good is that for the birds?

Now in the counsel of prayer it is hard to picture anyone who only has received, found, and walked through openings. Some people do try to twist this by saying that if we ask for the wrong thing God gives and we receive, or that we may think God has not answered, when God has, but not in congenial ways. Perhaps that is comforting to some. I do not find it contributing much to the description of God in action, the God of steadfast love. Let each of you go your own way on that; I'll live with the unfinishedness and the mystery, and let "the morrow" find God explaining it.

I mention all this because this passage on prayer is likely to evoke from each of us somewhat different responses. If tried out in a group, this will become obvious at once. For some, God's providence is discernible and identifiable up close and instantly. Terrorists kill 250 people and four survive. Relatives of these appear at once on television and respond, when an interviewer asks them, that their being spared is a sign of God's goodness and favor; God "wanted them to live" for a special purpose. I turn off the set in sympathy with the grieving families of the 250 whose mourning is made worse, whose explanations are more inexplicable, thanks to such theology. Once again, I'd leave this in the realm of what Luther reminds us is to be called "chance"—and do the theological interpreting in the light of chance. But, I plead with the individual reader or the group alike: don't take my word for it, and don't think that I think I've already thought this elusive question through to anyone's satisfaction, beginning with my own.

So, we are to ask, and it will be given. The line prompts Luther to offer a discourse on prayer, which he rates second only to preaching. He has introduced it by telling us that all Jesus has said about the ways and promises of God will fail to have full effect unless we respond in prayer. (Thinking back to our essay on the meaning of conversation: conversation with God, with the Jesus of the Sermon on the Mount is prayer; conversation among humans or with texts is interpretation.)

Luther speaks of the counsel to pray as an admonition. Here is a warning: pray, or else. "Or else it makes me afraid that some great misfortune which we could have prevented will overtake us." Luther obviously has a stronger sense of Providence being moved to change earthly things thanks to the act of praying than I do. Readers may find themselves positioned anywhere on the spectrum that spans the gap from "chance" to "foreordained."

Now we get a bit of folkloric expression. Luther knows that some peasants pay grain to the minister, the professional who then prays for him. He knows of those who depend on nonprofessionals who are observedly busy enough with prayer that they keep God's ears filled and God does not need "my" prayer. We all pray because of the command and promise, or at least we do in Luther's book.

Next he turns familial, following along with the text of the Sermon on the Mount. We fallible humans don't hand scorpions to good-for-nothing sons. If that is the case, how much better will the Creator treat us. "Your" nature is blighted and without a single good trait in comparison with God, so God, "whose nature is entirely good" will give the good things.

Realism re-enters when Luther recognizes enemies to the life of prayer. We become "bored, inattentive, and indifferent" to the Word of God and the good life. We lack wisdom, faith, love, and patience. We get dragged from the center of grace by the devil as first enemy and the world as the second. He thinks one has to practice to become a kind of virtuoso in the life of prayer. He advises practices: in anguish or need, drop to the knees and pray. Then there is no need to torture one's self. "This is a very precious medicine."

Luther has to answer something that may inspire our curiosity: why speak three times . . . ask, seek, knock. The repetition was there to pull us from timid thoughts and doubts. Be sure that you really believe in Christ and have a proper occupation, he has urged. Luther is so strong about this that he twice quotes James 5:16-17, a chapter from his least favorite ("right strawy") New Testament book to make the point. James counsels persistence: keep knocking. This is only a test, Luther says. But it teaches that prayer is not displeasing or unheard. "You are permitted to go on seeking and knocking."

I think of Jesus in the Garden of Gethsemane the night before his death. He prayed that the cup of suffering be taken from him by his father. It was not. Did that lead to a resigned last word, "Thy will be done?" In other words, Father, you are bigger than I am and you won't give me what I want, so I will give in and give up. No, one of the Gospels has him do the asking, not getting the receiving, but he kept on praying anyhow. Prayer is part of a continuing conversation with God that, in Jesus' case and certainly Luther's and most certainly in ours, does not depend upon how many possessions and other gifts each gets.

Reflection questions

1. Asking, seeking, and knocking are equated with praying in this section of the Sermon on the Mount. How do you know what to ask for? How do you know when to knock?

2. Discerning the "answers" to prayers can be challenging, if not confusing. What have you experienced regarding answered or unanswered prayer?

3. We are encouraged to come to God in confidence, expecting to receive what we need. Jesus himself came seeking to avoid the cup of suffering, but God's answer was the cross. What do you make of that?

4. Some would say that the reason why we don't have more "success" or receive "more blessings" is that we do not ask for or seek them often enough or diligently enough. How do you respond to such thinking?

5. Take some time to think about your own life of asking, seeking, and knocking. Would you change anything about your prayer life? Why?

4

When You Pray

And when you pray, you must not be like the hypocrites; for they love to stand and pray in the synagogues and at the street corners, that they may be seen by men. Truly, I say to you, they have their reward. But when you pray, go into your room and shut the door and pray to your Father who is in secret; and your Father who sees in secret will reward you. (6:5-6)

Luther: Here the emphasis is on the fact that (petition) must be a genuine prayer and not a piece of hypocrisy. . . . Therefore, in instructing them how to pray correctly, Christ begins by showing them how they should go about it: they are not supposed to stand and pray publicly on the streets, but they should pray at home, in their own room, alone, in secret. This means that, above all, they should rid themselves of the false motive of praying for the sake of the appearance or reputation or anything of that sort. It does not mean that prayer on the street or in public is prohibited; for a Christian is not bound to any particular place and may pray anywhere, whether he is on the street or in the field or in church. All it means is that this must not be done out of regard for other people, as a means of getting glory or profit. In the same way He does not forbid the blowing of a trumpet or the ringing of a bell at almsgiving for its own sake, but He denounces the addition of a false motivation when He says: "in order to be seen by men."

Nor is it a necessary part of this commandment that you have to go into a room and lock yourself in. Still, it is a good idea for a person to be alone when he intends to pray, so that he can pour out his prayer to God in a free and uninhibited manner, using words and gestures that he could not use if he were in human company. Although it is true that prayer can take place in the heart without any words or gestures, yet such things help in stirring up and enkindling the spirit even more; but in addition, the praying should continue in the heart almost without interruption. As we have said, a Christian always has the Spirit of supplication with him, and his heart is continually sending forth sighs and petitions to God, regardless of whether he happens to be eating or drinking or working. For his entire life is devoted to spreading the name of God, His glory, and His kingdom, so that whatever else he may do has to be subordinated to this.

Nevertheless, I say, outward prayer must also go on, both individual prayer and corporate prayer. In the morning and in the evening, at table and whenever he has time, every individual should speak a benediction or the Our Father or the Creed or a psalm. And in assemblies the Word of God should be employed and thanks and petitions voiced to God for our general needs. This must necessarily be done in public, with a special time and place set aside for such assemblies. Such prayer is a precious thing and a powerful defense against the devil and his assaults. For in it, all Christendom combines its forces with one accord; and the harder it prays, the more effective it is and the sooner it is heard. . . . Thus it is certain that whatever still stands and endures, whether it is in the spiritual or in the secular realm, is being preserved through prayer.

(I shall only summarize . . . briefly here) the component parts and the characteristics which every real prayer has to possess. . . . They are as follows: first, the urging of God's commandment, who has strictly required us to pray; second, His promise, in which He declares that He will hear us; third, an examination of our own need and misery, which burden lies so heavily on our shoulders that we have to carry it to God immediately and pour it out before Him, in accordance with His order and commandment; fourth, true faith, based on this word and promise of God, praying with the certainty and confidence that He will hear and help us—and all these things in the name of Christ, through whom our prayer is acceptable to the Father and for whose sake He gives us every grace and every good.

Christ indicates this by His use of one word when He says: "Pray to your Father who is in secret"; and later on He makes it even more explicit when He says: "Our Father who art in heaven." For this is the same as teaching that our prayer should be addressed to God as our gracious and friendly father, not as a tyrant or an angry judge. Now, no one can do this unless he has a word of God which says that He wants to have us call Him "Father" and that as a father He has promised to hear us and help us. To do this, one must also have such a faith in his heart and a happy courage to call God his Father, praying on the basis of a hearty confidence, relying upon the certainty that the prayer will be heard, and then waiting for help. . . .

. . . Learn, therefore, that there can be no real prayer without this faith. But do you feel weak and fearful? Your flesh and blood is always putting obstacles in the way of faith, as if you were not worthy enough or ready enough or earnest enough to pray. Or do you doubt that God has heard you, since you are a sinner? Then hold on to the Word and say: "Though I am sinful and unworthy, still I have the commandment of God, telling me to pray, and His promise that He will graciously hear me, not on account of my worthiness, but on account of the Lord Christ." In this way you can chase away the thoughts and the doubts, and you can cheerfully kneel down to pray. You need not consider whether you are worthy or unworthy; all you need to consider is your need and His Word, on which He tells you to build. This is especially so because He has set before you the manner of praying and put into your mouth the words you are to use when you pray, as follows here. Thus you may joyfully send up these prayers through Him and put them into His bosom, so that through His own merit He may bring them before the Father.

Marty: Fine. In these words from the Sermon on the Mount Jesus has us all poised to pray when Martin Luther, our guide, risks getting us off the track by pointing to a possible barrier: hypocrisy. It is hard to picture praying without some mixture of motives, but the notion that we might fall into hypocrisy while doing so is a nerve-wracking notion. The mixture of motives comes about because prayer is supposed to involve love of God, reliance on God, wanting God's will and way to be done—and yet it is also supposed to involve our needs. When do those needs become so strong that they block out all others? And when do they seem so compelling that, in attending to them, we think we have to adopt the right posture before God. And since we don't always have it in our hearts to have that posture, there is a temptation that we will fake it.

Maybe we will deceive the person near us, who is supposed to notice how fervent and devoted we are, so that she will think better of us. Maybe we will deceive ourselves, since it is possible to go through the motions of something without having the heart in them, and hoping that the actions, the motions themselves, will do good. The third party, God, is not likely to be deceived by hypocrisy.

Still, we are left with the task of sorting out sincerities from hypocrisies. That is hard to do with other people. Is that politician sincere when he calls us to pray and poses for the camera, praying? Or is he bidding for favor and votes? Is that pastor, whose faults we so well know, sincere in asking us to join in prayer, touting the efficacy of prayer—even though we know that pastor's a worrier who does not turn everything over to God? It turns out that people who do not care for a politician or her politics are inclined to find hypocrisy, while those who associate their political views with that politician thank God for her manifest sincerity. Those who have been well served by a sacrificial pastor will be sure that the pastor's call to prayer is sincere, while someone who feels snubbed or hangs out with gossips is ready to believe the worst.

"Here the emphasis is on the fact that petition must be a genuine prayer and not a piece of hypocrisy." Maybe the thing to do is not worry about being authentic or being hypocritical, and just try on for size the act of praying. Do it, and sincerity will follow. Luther is not quite content with that, as he points out how Christ here does need to give praying lessons, and we need to learn them.

Right off, we find that it is the word of Christ, not the comment of Luther that has us focus on hypocrisy. Here as so often in the Gospels, we get overtones of controversies Jesus was having with religious authorities, and sometimes even bold and blatant denunciations. He knew what was in the heart of those who opposed him, and he had eyes to see how they went about deceiving others.

We have to fit this denunciation of hypocrites into the larger picture of Jesus at work. Someone has pointed out that Jesus had only one liturgical reform in mind. He was not a member of a commission charged to write a new hymn and service book. There is no evidence that he cared how one turned to the altar, and whether the one who prays should fold hands with fingers interlocked or together. You would not consult the words of Jesus in the Gospels to learn how long the fringes on prayer shawls should be. You find him busy always, only, doing one thing.

That one thing was reforming the life of prayer, making it free of charge, unencumbered, unfussy. If Mary and Joseph could get away with a sacrifice of "a pair of turtle doves or two young pigeons," because that was stated in the law (Luke 2:24), how can we be sure that parents throughout Galilee and Judea could afford even such an expensive gift for God, or how can we be sure that they were all healthy enough to go out and catch doves or pigeons? What mattered to Jesus, as we learn in many Gospel references, was not whether one was rich enough to bring even a small gift, or smart enough to know the law about sacrifice. Jesus simply wanted people to be free to pray, to talk to the Father without mediation, professional intervention, or the need to hire public relations experts.

We poise ourselves, then, in the company of those who read and hear these words. The temptation for the politician or the celebrity to be the picture of piety is strong, and the pictures of him or her in the act of praying can be very useful to publics who favor prayer and piety. But who is watching us? Who cares? A person at the other end of the pew? The person who looks up and peeks a bit in a prayer circle, to see whether all the others in that circle are concentrating on the prayer or showing off by their attendance? There is no reason for most of us to care all that much about being observed as prayerfully pious. But these words, we believe, were not prepared to give a picture of how bad the synagogue prayer people are, but for us to examine ourselves, ready ourselves, and put most into and get most out of the act of praying.

Sometimes these words from long ago resonate in the controversies of our own day. It happens that our culture and society are often torn by issues over the public character of prayer. No one is critical, indeed almost everyone is happy, if on our walls, in our homes, and on our lawns, there are the marks of private prayer: a creche on the lawn, a cross on the wall, a scroll of the ten commandments on a sanctuary wall. But often we read of communities torn apart because one religious group, almost always Christian of one sort or another, wants the particular symbols of a particular faith to be represented and even to dominate on public grounds. Understandable as the impulse to have one's own prayer to one's own God given visible status, as controversies among the various religions and nonreligions sunder a community, the question rises: Is this all about praying to God—it may be, let's grant it—or is it more about who used to run the country and feels squeezed now. Or about who belongs and who doesn't. And who knows that you can "use" prayer as a kind of public utility: there is a waterworks, so why not a "prayerworks," something that is supposed to produce morality. Could it be—I will not answer the question I am posing— that the defenders of the Christian symbol on the public grounds, or the insisting on prayer when the faithful and the faithless both gather, is the kind of thing Jesus wants us to ask questions about?

For Luther, the words of Jesus mean "that, above all, (disciples) are not supposed to stand and pray publicly in the streets." Jesus himself did not only pray in his "own room, alone, in secret," we have read that we should. He prayed in a garden, at lakeside, above the city. What matters for us is not locale but motive. Disciples "should rid themselves of the false motive of praying for the sake of the appearance or reputation or anything of that sort." We read that prayer on the street or in public is prohibited; Luther is not talking about legal prohibition, but divine strictures. No, a Christian may pray anywhere, in field or street or even "in church."

The point is clear: the act cannot mean praying if it is done for notice by others, for glory, for profit. There is even support here for blowing trumpets and ringing bells, if that makes the donor happy in giving gifts. I suppose this could mean that Christians celebrating a festival or an anniversary or a rally could be out on the church lawn or marching down a street making all the noise they want. Once again: what matters is "false motivation," since, it is emphasized, one is likely to do all this "in order to be seen by men."

Good sense prevails as we read also that it is not commanded that the one who would pray should lock himself into a room. Instead, good sense dictates that we notice how people go about concentrating. Being alone for some prayer is liberating: the one who prays can be "free and uninhibited," which is evidently the only way to catch on to what prayer is: an open conversation. In public there are reasons to be inhibited; it is possible that others will be embarrassed if the one who prays flails around with wild gestures. Gestures can stir up emotions and heat up the spirit; well and good. But so long as prayer issues from the quiet chamber of a heart, it interferes with no one and calls for no attention except from the ear and mind of God.

Picture prayer in this context as more of that conversation between the believer and God. Luther draws on Romans 8 here, reminding us that the Christian is always emitting signals and sighs to God, even when not adopting postures of prayer, speaking in set language, or any language at all. You can eat or drink or work, it says here, and be praying while doing so. The Spirit, said Paul in Romans 8:26-27, gives utterance, and pleads for the person who, for example, eats and drinks and works in good faith.

The language of praying in private can be almost too popular today, and those who pick up these words from the Sermon on the Mount need to put them in context, a context Luther provides. As quickly as he has taken believers from the public to the closet or the chamber of the heart, he reminds himself to pull them out into public life again. For many, prayer now means "spirituality." Somehow they come to believe that they can avoid hypocrisy and hypocrites by avoiding the gatherings of the faithful. Today that gets called avoiding "organized religion" or "the institutional church." Today that private spirituality gets higher marks. You will find it being exercised as individuals read books of mysticism or spirituality while sipping on a cup of latté in the coffee corner of a giant bookstore. One meditates, sips, and goes out alone into the night.

That is not enough, for what Luther calls "outward prayer" also has its place, "both individual prayer and corporate prayer." He gives lessons to corroborate and reinforce what he takes from the words in the Gospel, and suggests some disciplines still worthy of following. He knew enough about psychology and distraction to know that believers would not put enough into prayer, or get enough out of it, if they did not take pains to set up routines for its practice. Yes, the Spirit prays with sighs we do not even hear. But fulfilled prayer does also occur with explicit words, among gatherings. The prescription is morning and evening and table prayer with a dash of more whenever one has time. Whoever cannot make up the words of conversation can use the Our Father or the Creed or a Psalm.

That is still not enough. In public assemblies at special times and places, prayer erupts. Picture more than a billion humans praying in such settings, for then "all Christendom combines its forces with one accord." Luther is so sure of the effects of prayer that he pictures society and the church imploding or crumbling without it. "Whether it is in the spiritual or in the secular realm," anything that stands and endures does so because it is "preserved through prayer." That is an astonishing and foolish-sounding claim. The towers of the Soviet Union stood and endured even though citizens were not allowed to pray in public. And some very Christian places where prayer goes on all the time do not stand and endure. What we find pictured here is that prayer, rising from gatherings of believers, belongs to the very structure and foundation of church and world. God sustains everything by the word of God's power—and is generous enough to include the response to that word by praying people, co-upholders, now.

It is impressive to see both how simple and how complex prayer can be. Our commentator wants to be helpful by boiling it all down to four elements. "Every real prayer" possesses these. They provide a good checklist for any of us who wonder whether what we are doing is really praying, or just going through motions. Here they are:

1. Prayer is the following of the commandment to pray. Whether anyone feels like praying or not, whether one is busy or idle, happy or sad, a creature of habit or someone who does things spontaneously, she converses with God because God commands it. "Talk to me!" we hear from the one Jesus calls Father. God intends a conversation, not a monologue. Like all the commandments, this one does not come up for any reason but to effect the connection between a God who is praised and ready and a believer who has need and gets to gain a hearing.

2. That leads to a second element: one prays because God promises to hear and answer. The word "promise" is almost a translation for the word "gospel" here as so often. The command means not that we have got to pray so much as that we get to pray. Promise comes from the words *pro* + *missio*, something that is pushed and projected into a world of mission and action. God gets committed to follow through with promise, as the believer in trust comes to God.

3. There has to be a ready heart, prepared to begin to understand what God gives in prayer, or what God withholds, or what God

gives in forms unanticipated. The picture here is of people so burdened by awareness of what they did wrong before God and others that they cannot function well. Prayer is the place where the believer dumps everything on God. Sometimes we call it "repentance." Here it gets called the act of carrying burdens to God and pouring them out.

4. All this must occur in the context of faith, of confidence that every prayer will be heard. The case here is that God will hear and help because promises go with the One who teaches us about prayer, Christ, whose life and death make our doing acceptable.

These four elements add up to prayer or provide the context for understanding what prayer is and does. The reason the believer confidently prays is because he has confidence in the character of God. It is not possible to comprehend all of God's mysterious action, but it is possible and urgent to get a sense of who God is. In the hearing of Jesus in his time and Luther in his, some counsel to pray stressed how powerful and formidable was the God before whom we are to have awe. Awe, yes; prostration before God, yes. But the awe and prostration get shown in front of a God who is "not a tyrant or an angry judge."

Instead this God is one who wants believers to call him "Father." I'd like to think that we are far enough along in talking about gender and language not to have to spend much time defending the biblical use of the term Father for God. Of course, the search for proper language about God will continue through the ages, just as it did through the centuries when the Bible was being written. Also, of course, for a half century now it has been important for not only women but all who would penetrate biblical witness to recognize that old translations and old readings and understanding often miss the point. The accent here is not on the maleness of God.

A colleague who has studied the Hebrew Bible well argues that the human mind is not capable of sustaining an imageless image of God. Instead, the Bible is full of anthropomorphism. Talk to someone, as one does in prayer, and it becomes necessary and even inevitable to be talking about ears, the countenance of God, the face of God, the mighty arm of God. But my friend says of all this, the Torah, the holy book, was written by people who did not have any interest in God below the waist line. That's not quite true, because some biblical pictures have God walking, which means having legs. None of them believed that God had legs literally. So if God is Father, this does not mean that God is reduced to human maleness.

I recall an afternoon in a divinity school, early in what gets called "the woman's revolution" or the movement toward gender equality and freedom, at a time when male symbols of God who both lacks and encompasses the features of what it is to be human, were irritants for many women. A noted feminist theologian had spoken and the then controversial or, admit it, still controversial question of feminine words for God came up. Should Christians who pray jettison words like Jesus' "Abba!" which is an intimate name for God. God as Father, some argued, has to go. The speaker admitted to the inherited problems with the term, and then questioned all alternatives. She was teaching the room that the fatherly picture of God is not the only way to speak about God.

After 45 minutes of give and take, it was time for her to summarize. She urged that all believers, in their congregations, walk through an exercise similar to the one we had just done, which was to relativize or color masculine names and pronouns for God and be free of what were then called sexist interpretations or instinctive applications of such to daily life. Then she said, "If you have been listening well to me, I think you are ready to join me in a prayer that will begin, "Loving Father." I think we were ready, and it is as hard to picture us praying it with the old connotations, just as it is possible to picture that we all learned how to pray it with new and broader ones, still saying "Our Father."

As often, as always, the whole accent when Luther speaks is on faith, and here he steps aside for counsel. He is likely that something or other—weakness, fear, a sense of unworthiness, an ability to be earnest enough—will block the path of prayer. He, perhaps more than most who pray today, had an intense consciousness of his flaws, his guilt. He could bore his confessor through six-hour recitations of faults too petty, his confessor would tell him, for God to care about. So now he pictures that the one who prays feels too unworthy to be in on the divine conversation. Forget it. Briskly, the comment moves on: pray because you are commanded to and you know you will be heard, because the Father is really hearing the Lord Christ praying with us, for us, through us, in our stead. The only requirement is a sense of need, or just plain need, whether we sense it all the time or not. If we bring an awareness of need, the prayer that follows will be joyful.

The privilege of talking directly to the Father, with no need for trumpets or bells or mediators, has reason to inspire joy and a sense of intimacy. Such prayer cannot be "used." Former White House press secretary and later television figure Bill Moyers in one of his books tells of an occasion when he was at the ranch and the Thanksgiving dinner table of President Lyndon Baines Johnson. Moyers was asked to pray, and began to do so, evidently not quite loudly enough for the President, at the far end of the table and with perhaps slightly dulled hearing, to hear. The President bellered that Moyers should speak louder, because he could not be heard. Respectfully, but with a smile, the press secretary looked up and, as if with a wink, said, "I was not talking to you, sir."

That makes for a nice story, though it does not cover all the bases. Prayer for those around a table represents those gathered, and they have a right to hear. But the basic point is: prayer is not directed to hosts, heads of tables, and people who lean forward, hands folded and noses assaulted by the wonderful aromas of readied food, but to the Giver.

Reflection questions

1. Neither Jesus nor Luther was not opposed to all public prayer. But what warning is sounded regarding the nature of praying in public?

2. What, or who, is to be the focus of prayer?

3. Review the four comments regarding prayer listed on pp. 71-72. Briefly summarize the way each adds to the "picture" of true prayer. Comment on any of these out of your experience of prayer.

4. Complete the following in as many ways as you wish: "When I pray I . . .

5

The Lord's Prayer

And in praying do not heap up empty phrases as the Gentiles do; for they think that they will be heard for their many words. Do not be like them, for your Father knows what you need before you ask him. Pray, then, like this:

> *Our Father who art in heaven,*
> *Hallowed be thy name.*
> *Thy kingdom come,*
> *Thy will be done, on earth as it is in heaven.*
> *Give us this day our daily bread;*
> *And forgive us our debts, as we also have forgiven our debtors;*
> *And lead us not into temptation,*
> *But deliver us from evil.*
> *[For thine is the kingdom and the power and the glory, forever.*
> *Amen.]*

   ⟨⟩ *Matthew 6:7-13*

Luther: . . . The Christian's prayer is easy, and it does not cause hard work. For it proceeds in faith on the basis of the promise of God, and it presents its need from the heart. Faith quickly gets through telling what it wants; indeed, it does so with a sigh that the heart utters and that words can neither attain nor express. As Paul says (Rom. 8:26), "the Spirit prays." And because He knows that God is listening to Him, He has no need of such everlasting twaddle. That is how the saints prayed in the Scriptures, like Elijah, Elisha, David, and others—with brief but strong and powerful words. This is evident in the Psalter, where there is hardly a single psalm that has a prayer more than five or six verses long. Therefore the ancient fathers have said correctly that many long prayers are not the way. They recommend short, fervent prayers, where one sighs toward heaven with a word or two, as is often quite possible in the midst of reading, writing, or doing some other task.

But the others, who make it nothing but a work of drudgery, can never pray with gladness or with devotion. They are glad when they are finally through with their babbling. And so it must be. Where there is no faith and no feeling of need in a petition, there the heart cannot be involved either. But where the heart is not involved and the body has to do all the work, there it becomes difficult drudgery. This is evident even in physical work. How difficult and dreary it is for the person who is doing something unwillingly! But on the other hand, if the heart is cheerful and willing, then it does not even notice the work. So it is here, too: the man who is serious in his intentions and takes pleasure in prayer neither knows nor feels any toil and trouble; he simply looks at his need, and he has finished singing or praying the words before he has a chance to turn around. In other words, prayers ought to be brief, frequent, and intense. For God does not ask how much and how long you have prayed, but how good the prayer is and whether it proceeds from the heart.

Therefore Christ says now: "Your heavenly Father knows what you need before you ask for it." It is as if He would say: "What are you up to? Do you suppose that you will talk Him down with your long babbling and make Him give you what you need? There is no need for you to persuade Him with your words or to give Him detailed instructions; for He knows beforehand what you need, even better than you do yourself." If you came before a prince or a judge who knew your case better than you could describe it to him and tried to give him a long-winded account of it, he would have a perfect right to laugh at you or, more likely, to become displeased with you. Indeed, as St. Paul says (Rom. 8:26), "We do not know how we are to pray." Therefore when He hears us, whatever He gives us is something in excess of our understanding or our hopes. Sometimes He lets us go on asking for something which He does not give right away, or perhaps does not give at all, knowing very well what is necessary and useful for us and what is not. We ourselves do not see this, but finally we have to admit that it would not have been good for us if He had done His giving on the basis of our petition. Therefore we must not go into a long harangue to give Him instructions or prescriptions about what He should do for us and how He should do it. He intends to give in such a way that His name might be hallowed, His kingdom extended, and His will advanced.

But you may say: "Since He knows and sees all our needs better than we do ourselves, why does He let us bring our petitions and present our need, instead of giving it to us without our petitioning? After all, He freely gives the whole world so much good every day, like the sun, the rain, crops and money, body and life, for which no one asks Him or thanks Him. He knows that no one can get along for a single day without light, food, and drink. Then why does He tell us to ask for these things?"

The reason He commands it is, of course, not in order to have us make our prayers an instruction to Him as to what He ought to give us, but in order to have us acknowledge and confess that He is already bestowing many blessings upon us and that He can and will give us still more. By our praying, therefore, we are instructing ourselves more than we are Him. It makes me turn around so that I do not proceed as do the ungodly, neither acknowledging this nor thanking Him for it. When my heart is turned to Him and awakened this way, then I praise Him, thank Him, take refuge with Him in my need, and expect help from Him. As a consequence of all this, I learn more and more to acknowledge what kind of God He is. Because I seek and knock at His door (Matt. 7:7), He takes pleasure in giving me ever more generous gifts. You see, that is how a genuine petitioner proceeds. He is not like those other useless babblers, who prattle a great deal but who never recognize all this. He knows that what he has is a gift of God, and from his heart he says: "Lord, I know that of myself I can neither produce nor preserve a piece of my daily bread; nor can I defend myself against any kind of need or misfortune. Therefore I shall look to Thee for it and request it from Thee, since Thou dost command me this way and dost promise to give it to me, Thou who dost anticipate my every thought and sympathize with my every need."

You see, a prayer that acknowledges this truly pleases God. It is the truest, highest, and most precious worship which we can render to Him; for it gives Him the glory that is due Him. The others do not do this. Like pigs, they grab all the gifts of God and devour them. They take over one country or city or house after another. They never consider whether they should be paying attention to God. Meanwhile they lay claim to holiness, with their many loud tones and noises in church. But a Christian heart is one that learns from the Word of God that everything we have is from God and nothing is from ourselves. Such a heart accepts all this in faith and practices it, learning to look to Him for everything and to expect it from Him. In this way praying teaches us to recognize who we are and who God is, and to learn what we need and where we are to look for it and find it. The result of this is an excellent, perfect, and sensible man, one who can maintain the right relationship to all things.

Having denounced and rejected . . . false and useless prayers, Christ now proceeds to introduce an excellent and brief formula. It shows how we are to pray and what we are to pray for. It includes all sorts of needs which ought to impel us to pray and of which we can daily remind ourselves with these short words. There is no excuse for anyone now, as though he did not know how or what to pray. Hence it is a very good practice . . . to pray the entire Lord's Prayer every day, morning and evening and at table, and otherwise, too, as a way of presenting all sorts of general needs to God. . . .

As has often been said . . . this is certainly the very best prayer that ever came to earth or that anyone could ever have thought up. Because God the Father composed it through His Son and placed it into His mouth, there is no need for us to doubt that it pleases Him immensely. At the very beginning He warns us to remember both His command and His promise, in the word "Our Father." He it is who demands this glory from us, that we should put our petitions to Him, as a child does to its father. He also wants us to have the confidence that He will gladly give us what we need. Also included is the reminder that we should glory in being His children through Christ. And so we come, on the basis of His command and His promise, and in the name of Christ, the Lord; and we present ourselves before Him with all confidence.

Now the first, second, and third petitions deal with the highest benefits that we receive from Him. In the first place, because He is our Father, He should receive from us the glory that is due Him, and His name should be held in high esteem throughout the world. By this petition I pile up on one heap every kind of false belief and worship, all of hell, and all sin and blasphemy. And I ask Him to put a stop to . . . all . . . who . . . desecrate and profane His name or seek their own glory under the pretext of His name. This is indeed only a brief phrase, but its meaning extends as far as the world and opposes all false doctrine and life.

In the second place, once we have His Word, true doctrine, and true worship, we also pray that His kingdom may be in us and remain in us; that is, that He may govern us in this doctrine and life, that He may protect and preserve us against all the power of the devil and his kingdom, and that He may shatter all the kingdoms that rage against His kingdom, so that it alone may remain. And in the third place, we pray that neither our will nor any other man's will, but His will alone may be done, and that what He plans and counsels may succeed and overcome all the schemes and undertakings of the world, as well as anything else that may set itself against His plans and counsels, even though the whole world were to mass itself and rally all its strength to defend its cause against Him. These are the three most important elements.

In the other four petitions we meet the needs that apply to our own daily life and to this poor, weak, and temporal existence.

Therefore our first petition here is that He may give us our daily bread—that is, everything necessary for the preservation of this life, like food, a healthy body, good weather, house, home, wife, children, good government, and peace—and that He may preserve us from all sorts of calamities, sickness, pestilence, hard times, war, revolution, and the like. Our next petition is this: that He may forgive us our debts and not look upon the shameful and thankless way we misuse the benefits with which He daily provides us in such abundance; that this may not prompt Him to deny us these benefits or to withdraw them or to punish us with the disfavor we deserve; but that He may graciously pardon us, although we who are called "Christians" and "children of God" do not live as we should. The third of these petitions is brought on by the fact that we are living on earth, amid all sorts of temptation and trouble, with attacks from every side. Thus the source of the hindrance and the temptation we experience is not only external, from the world and the devil, but also internal, from our own flesh. Amid so much danger and temptation, we cannot live the way we should; nor would we be able to stand it for a single day. We ask Him, therefore, to sustain us in the midst of this danger and need so that it does not overcome and destroy us. And our final petition is that He would ultimately deliver us completely from all evil, and when the time comes for us to pass out of this life, that He would bestow upon us a gracious and blessed hour of death. In this brief compass we have laid all our physical and spiritual needs into His lap, and each individual word has summarized an entire world of meaning.

But in the text there is a small addition with which He concludes the prayer, a sort of thanksgiving and common confession, namely this: "For Thine is the kingdom and the power and the glory, forever." These are really the titles and names that are appropriate to God alone, for these three things He has reserved for Himself—to govern, to judge, and to glory. No one has a right to judge or to rule or to have sovereignty except God alone, or those whom He has commissioned with it, those through whom, as His servants, He maintains His rule. In the same way, no man may exercise judgment over another, or become angry at him and punish him, unless he has the office to do so on God's behalf. For this is not a right innate in men, but one given by God. These are the two things that He names here: "the kingdom," that is, the sovereignty by which all authority is His; and then "the power," that is, the consequence of His authority, its execution, by which He can punish, subject the wicked to Himself, and protect the pious. For he who punishes is doing so in God's stead; all administering of justice, all protecting and preserving, is derived from His power. Therefore no one should wreak vengeance or exact punishment on his own; for it does not lie within his official capacity or ability, and it does not do any good either. As He says (Rom. 12:19): "Vengeance is mine, I will repay"; and elsewhere He threatens (Matt. 26:52): "All who take the sword for vengeance will be punished by the sword."

In the same way "the glory," or honor or praise, belongs only to God. No one may boast of anything, his wisdom or holiness or ability, except through Him and from Him. When I honor a king or a prince and call him "gracious lord" or bend my knee before him, I am not doing this to him on account of his own person but on account of God, to one who is sitting in majesty in God's stead. It is the same when I show honor to my father and mother or to those who are in their stead. I am not doing this to a human being but to a divine office, and I am honoring God in them. Wherever there is authority and power, therefore, the glory and the praise belong to Him. And so His kingdom, power, and glory prevail throughout the world. It is He alone that is ruling, punishing, and being glorified in the divine offices and stations, like those of father, mother, master, judge, prince, king, and emperor. The devil is opposing this through his minions. He himself is seeking to exercise the authority and power, to wreak the vengeance and exact the punishment, and to monopolize all the glory. That is why the petitions for His name, His kingdom, and His will are foremost here; for they alone must prevail, and all other names, kingdoms, powers, and wills must be shattered. Thus we acknowledge that He is supreme in all three of these areas, but that the others are His instruments, by which He acts to accomplish these things.

Marty: Even when we get to the Lord's Prayer, we do not get to the Lord's Prayer. The climax of all the verses here is the set of lines that have certainly been repeated more frequently by Christians than any other sequence, and yet it has to wait, while the Sermon on the Mount includes still more counsel from Jesus.

Here it is: don't heap up empty phrases. The other people, the Gentiles, the outsiders, do that. And they have a reason. They have been trained to think that God will hear them more readily if they go on and on and on. There seems to be a contradiction here: on one hand we are told to pray without ceasing, pray all the time, count on the Spirit to be praying for us with sighs that we may not hear or about which we may not think. And then here Jesus is heard being very abrupt: keep it short! Keep the prayers pointed and succinct.

Often in the Old Testament we find the Lord giving prescriptions so we understand how prayer connects with the rest of the believers' lives. It is possible to go through the motions to impress God and to overlook care for God's people. Turn to Isaiah 58 for an example. The Lord hears the people of Israel (not the Gentiles!) proclaiming that they are seeking God and delighting to know the ways of the Lord. They fast, and fast, and complain that God is not impressed and does not answer prayers. Then comes the stern word that matches Jesus' word about blowing the trumpets for public prayer: You fast, says the Lord, until you quarrel and fight and get hungry and therefore angry and you beat up on each other (see verse 4). Is that what the Lord wanted?

The Lord wanted the people to save time to do his will by loosening the bonds of injustice, undoing the thongs of yokes and thus liberating others, sharing bread with the hungry and sheltering the homeless poor in their own houses, covering the naked, and taking care of their own relatives. Those were acts of prayer that God would rightfully notice, and after which "your light shall break forth like the dawn, and your healing shall spring up quickly" (58:9, NRSV). God would be present among them.

In the Sermon on the Mount Jesus gives a new additional reason to get to the heart of things: the Father knows already what you need before you ask him. Praying with that in mind, says our commentator, "does not cause hard work." Prayer in faith quickly gets past what the one who is praying wants, and then turns over to the Spirit the constant praying. There is therefore, we have read, "no need for such everlasting twaddle" as long, impressive prayers represent. Luther hauls out a phone book full of saints who got right to the point: Elijah, Elisha, David, "and others" who used brief and powerful words. He is not as good at mathematics as at roll call, claiming as he does that there is "hardly a single psalm that has a prayer more than five or six verses long." Maybe he is accurate, if one wants to separate out the specific words of prayer from other aspects of Psalm-language. In any case, the point is well taken: the best prayers remembered have the sense of direction and directness that we find in the Psalms. Flip them open to whatever page will lie flat and confront you, and you are likely to find this to be the case. He also cites the ancient fathers of the church, who caught the spirit of the Psalms and recommended short, fervent prayers, sometimes only a word or two long, things that can be uttered "in the midst of reading, writing, or doing some other task."

Luther really pours it on: long and repetitive prayers have already been called "twaddle" and now, in translation, they get called "drudgery" and "babbling." Such lines ought to be liberating to anyone who thinks that prayers have to be hard work.

Next, Luther turns into an expert on the psychology of work, noting something that we can likely corroborate in our experience and observation, for example of children. If you put your heart into something, you are not so eager to have it end as the twaddle and babbling drudges are when they finally get long prayers over with. This is the case with work. Those who put their heart into it and get involved, find it fulfilling, but where they do not or cannot, it is always and only difficult and dreary drudgery. If one's heart is cheerful and willing, "then it does not even notice the work."

Writing is work, and when I had to write editorial comment on scores of papers handed in by students, I found it easy to procrastinate and found the paper-correcting days very long. Let me hasten to add that I was blessed to get to correct very many good papers, and enjoyed that. But, still, such days were longer than those in which I got to write in creative ways. I mention that and the next autobiographical reference as check points or templates for you readers, to try the exercise yourself, and then apply it to work and praying.

As a high schooler, college bound, just under draft age near the end of the Second World War, I "did my part" by helping the war effort in a factory. I also did my part for myself, earning enough through six ten-hour days each week to make it possible for me not to have to work while at college. The routine work helped provide me with motive to find empathy for the millions who have such routine jobs. It also gave me the example of coworkers who endured, were generous, often funny, and exemplary in so many ways other than in their choice of salty vocabulary. But I could not visit with them and learn the bad words very often because the machines were noisy.

It was my task to countersink the eighteen holes for screws in the brake shoes of Sherman tanks. I would not have known a Sherman tank if it smashed through our factory, but I surely knew the holes at which I stared and which the drill press that I controlled attacked. Forty-five seconds was all I got to complete each, before another rolled by. One could not have heard a radio, so there was no stimulus.

Only the chart I put above the press, "Eighty-Five Days Left" and then "Eighty-Four Days Left" and the sight of the clock that dragged along toward coffee break and then lunch and then coke break and then quitting time inspired. The rest was "difficulty" and "dreary" and "drudgery"—exactly like prayer when one does not put her heart into it, according to the testimony of Luther.

I went into that detail in order to clear the way for the inspiration, the pleasure, the toil-free untroubled character of pointed prayer. Before the one who prays "has a chance to turn around," the prayers are over, because they are "brief, frequent, and intense." The test is not the length of the prayer but the heart of the pray-er. You do not have to persuade your Father to keep your needs in mind, is the next word. You will get laughed at, we are reminded, if you waste the time of a prince or judge who already knows your case. Come to the point. Keep it short. Cut that.

You may have some trouble—I do—with the idea that God may let us go on asking "for something which He does not give right away, or perhaps does not give at all," knowing what is necessary and useful for us and what is not. I have to confess that while I yield to God, who knows what I do not, I am not so ready to buy into the notion that I will always come to understand and agree with the way God answers. We do not have to understand or agree about, ever, what greater good came when a loved one for whose life we prayed prematurely died. We do not have to understand or agree with the plots of historical tales in which the righteous suffer, the innocent get raped, or the zealous go hungry. It is sometimes more helpful to say "that's how things are" than to have an explanation for the mysterious ways of God. But the words here are useful to the extent that they ask us only not to have to give God "instructions and prescriptions."

Ah, we are back to the psychology of the person who is to pray but keeps coming back with logic as the Sermon on the Mount goes on. It's logical to ask why, if God knows better than we do what we need and supplies it better than we could have imagined, what is the point of it all? "After all," God gives so much good every day whether we believe or not, pray or not, so why must we be commanded to bring our needs before him? Luther's answer, and it fits pretty well is this: our prayers are not the "instructions and prescriptions" that get ruled out, but means of stimulating our acknowledgment of their source. "By our praying, therefore, we are instructing ourselves more than we are Him." Prayer makes us turn around, to praise and to motivate us to find refuge. It's all a matter of acknowledging the Source of good, not of giving the Father directions.

The best sermon I ever heard on "The Ten Lepers" had this point: In the parable Jesus gave prescriptions to ten lepers. There was a promise that if they followed these and went through the proper ritual, they would be healed. All obeyed. All were healed. One, only one, came back to thank. The preacher said: "That was the church." A world can ignore blessings and their source, but it misses a lot. The healed leper who came back got more out of the experience than mere healing. Like the one who takes the lesson from Jesus in the Sermon on the Mount, as Luther points out, finds a new identity. Speaking to us together: praying "teaches us to recognize who we are and who God is." There's a new entry in Who's Who in the Kingdom: an "excellent, perfect, and sensible" person who "can maintain the right relationship to all things." It may take a lifetime to realize this, but that may be why we are to pray the Lord's Prayer daily, often. It may finally begin to sink in.

It may sound contradictory, after blasting repetitious and long prayer, for Luther to stress that it would be a good idea to pray the Lord's Prayer in the morning, in the evening, at the table, "and otherwise." He seems to see it invested with so much meaning that every time it gets prayed we will find something fresh in it, because it is "general" and "composed" by God through his son, so we know it has to be pleasing.

When he finally gets to the Prayer itself, Luther moves along and seems to want to move us along rather rapidly, as if it needed no explanation. In other contexts, he slows down. Thus in both of his catechisms he elaborates on the seven petitions individually, bringing up ideas worth consulting by anyone who wants to probe them more deeply. For now, he is our commentator, our conversation partner with the Jesus of the Sermon on the Mount, so he gets to set the agenda.

So the first, second, and third petitions in a way contain everything. The "Our Father, who art in heaven, hallowed be Thy name" phrase gives us the chance to "pile up on one heap every kind of false belief and worship," which means all that does not acknowledge this God and become aware of his perspective and care, which encompasses all. One can detect in Luther's remarks some signs that he was having battles over "false doctrine and life," battles which he found winnable with this petition before him. Not that there is not enough "false belief and worship" around, but most of us are likely to find other instruments to interpret and confront it. At the moment, before us is the value of acknowledging the God beyond the gods. Some of us could have wished that Luther would have left commentary and advice about "hallowing" in a world in which so little is sacred. But in a way that comes out in what follows, namely, a way of life centered in prayer and trust.

So Luther after eleven lines on the petition that has it all moves us on to the word, "Thy kingdom come." This sweeping prayer gets and needs only eight lines. The kingdom, which we began to define in an earlier chapter, is not something "out there" but, in this prayer, is also to "be in us and remain in us," so that it will be God and not ourselves or someone or something else that does the governing.

The third phrase, "They will be done on earth as it is in heaven," prompts a ten-line elaboration. Here is reference to the cosmic drama that it's God's will against all plans and counsels and schemes and undertakings of the world. As one mystical line put it: "In his will is our peace." Luther is almost that brief, but he puts his energy into seeing how this prayer, when answered, will thwart the will of those who work against that peace.

Now comes a break, since after talking to and about God, it is time to deal with "daily life and to this poor, weak, and temporal existence." Daily bread, for Luther here and in the Catechism, includes "food, a healthy body, good weather, house, home, wife, children, good government, and peace." He must have turned these over in his mind often, since similar catalogs turn up regularly in his catechisms and other writings. And he is just as busy cataloging what works against such daily bread: "all sorts of calamities, sickness, pestilence, hard times, war, revolution, and the like."

We might like to linger here a bit and pursue questions about what happens when bread as he defines it is scarce and calamities as he mentions them are abundant, but in a sense his whole treatment of the Sermon on the Mount is designed to address that.

"And forgive us our debts, as we also have forgiven our debtors." That petition is red meat for a ravenous Luther, a pole star to which he is directed and drawn and would draw us, the heart and core and glowing center of what everything else in positive divine-human relations are about. Someone wisely said that Luther's teachings do not come together like pearls on a string, so that we can cut one out and tie it back together and hardly notice the difference. No, they all radiate out from this core, like rays from the sun. No one will understand a point of his theology unless he can somehow correlate it with the good news of the forgiveness of sins. Luther's theology is not the current point; at present we are concerned to see how this prayer fits into the search for trust and the way of life that grows out of it.

There is not as much stress here as one would expect on the theme in this translation that has us praying for forgiveness as we have forgiven, except when our commentator reminds us that being called "Christians" and "children of God" means little if we do not live as we should, namely, as forgivers. And when we do not, we will not understand and realize all the benefits of divine forgiveness.

Instantly this comment on forgiveness ends and Luther follows the text to "And lead us not into temptation." He became a specialist at diagnosing the two kinds of temptations he mentions here: from without (world, devil, etc.) and from within (the flesh, and all that means). Through his many writings he often dwells on a word that does not translate well, *Anfechtungen*. These are the plaguing temptations that he sees as coming even from God, temptations that he says somewhere work curiously both to drive us from God and then pull us to God, in an embrace. We need all the help we can get, and this petition, prayed thoughtfully, helps provide it.

One more: "But deliver us from evil." Here the accent is not on being spared encounters with evil along life's way, but at its end, so that we experience "a gracious and blessed hour of death." The accent is on the deliverance that gets called "ultimate," but it shadows life all along the way, so the prayer gets directed to that, too.

Not all texts and versions of the Bible conclude the prayer with "for Thine is the kingdom and the power and the glory, forever." Sometimes in ecumenical gatherings we will hear half the congregation charging ahead through that extra line, while others are saying, "Amen." The commentator here likes the lines, because the prayer thus ends by giving God the proper titles and tasks: "to govern, to judge, and to glory." Whoever prays it is saying that no one else has a right to these except where God commissions it. He famously makes room for the authority of earthly governors, whom he considers as deputies of God, the only ones who have the right to exercise judgment or punish another. It is a plea that in the ordinary course of life no one, including those appointed to administer justice, can take vengeance into their own hands or punish others. So suddenly this word of glory gets converted into a "No Vengeance!" stipulation.

Finally, it ties this sense of derived authority to the giving of honor. Bend the knee before an earthly ruler and you are not bending the knee on his account but because of God's deputizing the person. Only God is to be honored. All other powers and kingdoms are to be shattered. That is not a point easily remembered among those with power, but in this interpretation, it stands before them as reminders and judgments.

The prayer ends with "Amen." No further comment needed.

For reflection

1. Reflect on Luther's comments about the directness of prayer. What seems to be the nature of effective prayers, as far as Luther is concerned?

2. Why does Luther encourage the frequent praying of the Lord's Prayer?

3. How do you respond to the following quote: "The test is not the length of the prayer but the heart of the pray-er"? How have you found this to be true in your experience?

4. How would you summarize the "purpose" of prayer? How is the Lord's Prayer an example of this purpose?

5. Consider reviewing the petitions of the Lord's Prayer in Luther's Small or Large Catechism. Share any new insights you discover there.

6. What new "learning" do you take from this chapter?

6

Blessed Are You

Blessed are the poor in spirit, for theirs is the kingdom of heaven.

Matthew 5:3

Luther: (Christ) does not come like Moses or a teacher of the Law, with demands, threats, and terrors, but in a very friendly way, with enticements, allurements, and pleasant promises. In fact, if it were not for this report which has preserved for us all the first dear words that the Lord Christ preached, curiosity would drive and impel everyone to run all the way to Jerusalem, or even to the end of the world, just to hear one word of it. You would find plenty of money to build such a road well! And everyone would proudly boast that he had heard or read the very word that the Lord Christ had preached. How wonderfully happy the man would seem who succeeded in this! That is exactly how it would really be if we had none of this in written form, even though there might be a great deal written by others. Everyone would say: "Yes, I hear what St. Paul and His other apostles have taught, but I would much rather hear what He Himself spoke and preached."

But now since it is so common that everyone has it written in a book and can read it every day, no one thinks of it as anything special or precious. Yes, we grow sated and neglect it, as if it had been spoken by some shoemaker rather than the High Majesty of heaven. Therefore it is in punishment for our ingratitude and neglect that we get so little out of it and never feel nor taste what a treasure, power, and might there is in the words of Christ. But whoever has the grace to recognize it as the Word of God rather than the word of man, will also think of it more highly and dearly, and will never grow sick and tired of it.

. . . Christ opens His mouth here and says that something is necessary other than the possession of enough on earth; as if He were to say: "My dear disciples, when you come to preach among the people, you will find out that this is their teaching and belief: 'Whoever is rich or powerful is completely blessed; on the other hand, whoever is poor and miserable is rejected and condemned before God.'" The Jews were firmly persuaded that if a man was successful, this was a sign that he had a gracious God, and vice versa. The reason for this was the fact that they had many great promises from God regarding the temporal, physical goods that He would grant to the pious. They counted upon these, in the opinion that if they had this, they were right with Him. The Book of Job is addressed to this theory. His friends argue and dispute with him about this and insist that he is being punished this way because of some great sin he must have knowingly committed against God. Therefore he ought to admit it, be converted, and become pious, that God might lift the punishment from him.

At the outset, therefore, it was necessary for His sermon to overthrow this delusion and to tear it out of their hearts as one of the greatest obstacles to faith and a great support for the idol Mammon in their heart. Such a doctrine could have no other consequence than to make people greedy, so that everyone would be interested only in amassing plenty and in having a good time, without need or trouble. And everyone would have to conclude: "If that man is blessed who succeeds and has plenty, I must see to it that I do not fall behind."

This is still what the whole world believes today. . . . (It) is the greatest and most universal belief or religion on earth. On it all men depend according to their flesh and blood, and they cannot regard anything else as blessedness. That is why He preaches a totally new sermon here for the Christians: If they are a failure, if they have to suffer poverty and do without riches, power, honor, and good days, they will still be blessed and have not a temporal reward, but a different, eternal one; they will have enough in the kingdom of heaven.

But you say: "What? Must all Christians, then, be poor? Dare none of them have money, property, popularity, power, and the like? What are the rich to do, people like princes, lords, and kings? Must they surrender all their property and honor, or buy the kingdom of heaven from the poor, as some have taught?" Answer: No. It does not say that whoever wants to have the kingdom of heaven must buy it from the poor, but that he must be poor himself and be found among the poor. It is put clearly and candidly, "Blessed are the poor." Yet the little word "spiritually" is added, so that nothing is accomplished when someone is physically poor and has no money or goods. Having money, property, land, and retinue outwardly is not wrong in itself. It is God's gift and ordinance. No one is blessed, therefore, because he is a beggar and owns nothing of his own. The command is to be "spiritually poor." . . . Christ is not dealing here at all with the secular realm and order, but that He wants to discuss only the spiritual— how to live before God, above and beyond the external. . . .

So be poor or rich physically and externally, as it is granted to you—God does not ask about this—and know that before God, in his heart, everyone must be spiritually poor. That is, he must not set his confidence, comfort, and trust on temporal goods, nor hang his heart upon them and make Mammon his idol. David was an outstanding king, and he really had his wallet and treasury full of money, his barns full of grain, his land full of all kinds of goods and provisions. In spite of all this he had to be a poor beggar spiritually, as he sings of himself (Ps. 39:12): "I am poor, and a guest in the land, like all my fathers." Look at the king, sitting amid such possessions, a lord over land and people; yet he does not dare to call himself anything but a guest or a pilgrim, one who walks around on the street because he has no place to stay. This is truly a heart that does not tie itself to property and riches; but though it has, it behaves as if it had nothing, as St. Paul boasts of the Christians (2 Cor. 6:10): "As poor, yet making many rich; as having nothing, and yet possessing everything."

All this is intended to say that while we live here, we should use all temporal goods and physical necessities, the way a guest does in a strange place, where he stays overnight and leaves in the morning. He needs no more than bed and board and dare not say: "This is mine, here I will stay." Nor dare he take possession of the property as though it belonged to him by right; otherwise he would soon hear the host say to him: "My friend, don't you know that you are a guest here? Go back where you belong." That is the way it is here, too. The temporal goods you have, God has given to you for this life. . . . You should not fasten or hang your heart on them as though you were going to live forever. You should always go on and consider another, higher, and better treasure, which is your own and which will last forever. . . .

Then, too, a man is called "rich" in Scripture, even though he does not have any money or property, if he scrambles and scratches for them and can never get enough of them. These are the very ones whom the Gospel calls "rich bellies," who in the midst of great wealth have the very least and are never satisfied with what God grants them. That is so because the Gospel looks into the heart, which is crammed full of money and property, and evaluates on the basis of this, though there may be nothing in the wallet or the treasury. On the other hand, it also calls a man "poor" according to the condition of his heart, though he may have his treasury, house, and hearth full. Thus the Christian faith goes straight ahead. It looks at neither poverty nor riches, but only at the condition of the heart. If there is a greedy belly there, the man is called "spiritually rich"; on the other hand, he is called "spiritually poor" if he does not depend upon these things and can empty his heart of them. As Christ says elsewhere (Matt. 19:29): "He who forsakes houses, land, children, or wife, will receive a hundredfold, and besides he will inherit eternal life." By this He seeks to rescue their hearts from regarding property as their treasure, and to comfort His own who must forsake it; even in this life they will receive more than they leave behind.

We are not to run away from property, house, home, wife, and children, wandering around the countryside as a burden to other people. . . . (Instead, this) is what it means: In our heart we should be able to leave house and home, wife and children. Even though we continue to live among them, eating with them and serving them out of love, as God has commanded, still we should be able, if necessary, to give them up at any time for God's sake. If you are able to do this, you have forsaken everything, in the sense that your heart is not taken captive but remains pure of greed and of dependence, trust, and confidence in anything. A rich man may properly be called "spiritually poor" without discarding his possessions. But when the necessity arises, then let him do so in God's name, not because he would like to get away from wife and children, house and home, but because, as long as God wills it, he would rather keep them and serve Him thereby, yet is also willing to let Him take them back.

So you see what it means to be "poor" spiritually and before God, to have nothing spiritually and to forsake everything. Now look at the promise which Christ appends when He says, "For of such is the kingdom of heaven." This is certainly a great, wonderful, and glorious promise. Because we are willing to be poor here and pay no attention to temporal goods, we are to have a beautiful, glorious, great, and eternal possession in heaven. And because you have given up a crumb, which you still may use as long and as much as you can have it, you are to receive a crown, to be a citizen and a lord in heaven. This would stir us if we really wanted to be Christians and if we believed that His words are true. But no one cares who is saying this, much less what He is saying. They let it go in one ear and out the other, so that no one troubles himself about it or takes it to heart.

With these words He shows that no one can understand this unless he is already a real Christian. This point and all the rest that follow are purely fruits of faith, which the Holy Spirit Himself must create in the heart. Where there is no faith, there the kingdom of heaven also will remain outside; nor will spiritual poverty, meekness,

and the like follow, but there will remain only scratching and scrap-
ing, quarrels and riots over temporal goods. Therefore it is all over
for such worldly hearts, so that they never learn or experience what
spiritual poverty is, and neither believe nor care what He says and
promises about the kingdom of heaven.

. . . This sermon does the world no good and accomplishes nothing for it. The world stubbornly insists upon being right. It refuses
to believe a thing, but must have it before its very eyes and hold it in
its hand, saying, "A bird in the hand is worth two in the bush."[6]
Therefore Christ also lets them go. He does not want to force anyone or drag him in by the hair. But He gives His faithful advice to
all who will let Him advise them, and He holds before us the dearest
promises. If you want it, you have peace and quiet in your heart here,
and hereafter whatever your heart desires forever. If you do not want
it, have your own way, and rather have sorrow and misfortune both
here and hereafter. For we see and experience that everything
depends upon being content and not clinging to temporal goods.
There are many people whose heart God can fill so that they may
have only a morsel of bread and yet are cheerful and more content
than any prince or king. In brief, such a person is a rich lord and
emperor, and he need have no worry, trouble, or sorrow. This is the
first point of this sermon: Whoever wants to have enough here and
hereafter, let him see to it that he is not greedy or grasping. Let him
accept and use what God gives him, and live by his labor in faith.
Then he will have Paradise and even the kingdom of heaven here, as
St. Paul also says (1 Tim. 4:8): "Godliness is of value in every way, as
it holds promise for the present life and also for the life to come."

Blessed are those who mourn, for they shall be comforted. (Matthew 5:4)

He began this sermon against the doctrine and belief of . . . the
whole world (which) even at its best . . . sticks to the delusion that
it is well off if it just has property, popularity, and its Mammon here,
and which serves God only for this purpose. In the same way He

now continues, overturning even what they thought was the best and most blessed life on earth, one in which a person would attain to good and quiet days and would not have to endure discomfort, as Psalm 73:5 describes it: "They are not in trouble as other men are; they are not stricken like other men."

For that is the highest thing that men want, to have joy and happiness and to be without trouble. Now Christ turns the page and says exactly the opposite; He calls "blessed" those who sorrow and mourn. Thus throughout, all these statements are aimed and directed against the world's way of thinking, the way it would like to have things. It does not want to endure hunger, trouble, dishonor, unpopularity, injustice, and violence; and it calls "blessed" those who can avoid all these things.

So He wants to say here that there must be another life than the life of their quests and thoughts, and that a Christian must count on sorrow and mourning in the world. Whoever does not want to do this may have a good time here and live to his heart's desire, but hereafter he will have to mourn forever. As He says (Luke 6:25): "Woe unto you that laugh and have a good time now! For you shall have to mourn and weep." This is how it went with the rich man in Luke 16. He lived luxuriously and joyfully all his life, decked out in expensive silk and purple. He thought he was a great saint and well off in the sight of God because He had given him so much property. Meanwhile he let poor Lazarus lie before his door daily, full of sores, in hunger and trouble and great misery. But what kind of judgment did he finally hear when he was lying in hell? "Remember that in your lifetime you received good things, but Lazarus evil things. Therefore you are now in anguish, but he is comforted" (Luke 16:25).

See, this is the same text as: "Blessed are those who mourn, for they shall be comforted," which is as much as saying, "Those who seek and have nothing but joy and fun here shall weep and howl forever."

You may ask again: "What are we to do, then? Is everyone to be damned who laughs, sings, dances, dresses well, eats, and drinks?

After all, we read about kings and saints who were cheerful and lived well. Paul is an especially wonderful saint; he wants us to be cheerful all the time (Phil. 4:4), and he says (Rom. 12:15): 'Rejoice with those who rejoice,' and again: 'Weep with those who weep.' That sounds contradictory, to be joyful all the time and yet to weep and mourn with others."

Answer: I said before that having riches is not sinful, nor is it forbidden. So also being joyful, eating and drinking well, is not sinful or damnable; nor is having honor and a good name. Still I am supposed to be "blessed" if I do not have these things or can do without them, and instead suffer poverty, misery, shame, and persecution. So both of these things are here and must be—being sad and being happy, eating and going hungry, as Paul boasts about himself (Phil. 4:11, 12): "I have learned the art, wherever I am, to be content. I know how to be abased, and I know how to abound; in any and all circumstances I have learned the secret of facing plenty and hunger, abundance and want." And in 2 Corinthians 6:8–10: "In honor and dishonor, in ill repute and good repute; as dying, and, behold, we live; as sorrowful, yet always rejoicing."

So this is what it means: A man is called "spiritually poor," not because he has no money or anything of his own, but because he does not covet it or set his comfort and trust upon it as though it were his kingdom of heaven. So also a man is said to "mourn and be sorrowful"—not if his head is always drooping and his face is always sour and never smiling; but if he does not depend upon having a good time and living it up, the way the world does, which yearns for nothing but having sheer joy and fun here, revels in it, and neither thinks nor cares about the state of God or men. . . .

Therefore mourning and sorrow are not a rare plant among Christians, in spite of outward appearances. They would like to be joyful in Christ, outwardly, too, as much as they can. Daily, whenever they look at the world, they must see and feel in their heart so much wickedness, arrogance, contempt, and blasphemy of God and

His Word, so much sorrow and sadness, which the devil causes in both the spiritual and the secular realm. Therefore they cannot have many joyful thoughts, and their spiritual joy is very weak. If they were to look at this continually and did not turn their eyes away from time to time, they could not be happy for a moment. It is bad enough that this really happens oftener than they would like, so that they do not have to go out looking for it.

Therefore simply begin to be a Christian, and you will soon find out what it means to mourn and be sorrowful. If you can do nothing else, then get married, settle down, and make a living in faith. Love the Word of God, and do what is required of you in your station. Then you will experience, both from your neighbors and in your own household, that things will not go as you might wish. You will be hindered and hemmed in on every side, so that you will suffer enough and see enough to make your heart sad. . . .

Because the world does not want to have such mourning and sorrow, it seeks out those stations and ways of life where it can have fun and does not have to suffer anything from anyone. . . . It cannot stand the idea that in a divine station it should serve other people with nothing but care, toil, and trouble, and get nothing as a reward for this but ingratitude, contempt, and other malicious treatment. Therefore, when things do not go with it as it wishes and one person looks at another with a sour face, all they can do is to batter things with cursing and swearing, and with their fists, too, and be ready to put up property and reputation, land and servants. But God arranges things so that they still cannot get off too easily, without seeing or suffering any trouble at all. What He gives them as a reward for not wanting to suffer is this: they still have to suffer, but by their anger and impatience they make it twice as great and difficult, and without finding any comfort or a good conscience. The Christians have the advantage that though they mourn, too, they shall be comforted and be blessed both here and hereafter. . . .

Those who mourn this way are entitled to have fun and to take it wherever they can so that they do not completely collapse for sorrow.

Christ also adds these words and promises this consolation so that they do not despair in their sorrow nor let the joy of their heart be taken away and extinguished altogether, but mix this mourning with comfort and refreshment. Otherwise, if they never had any comfort or joy, they would have to languish and wither away. No man can stand continual mourning. It sucks out the very strength and savor of the body, as the wise man says (Ecclus. 30:25): "Sadness has killed many people"; and again (Prov. 17:22): "A downcast spirit dries up the marrow in the bones." Therefore we should not neglect this but should command and urge such people to have a good time once in a while if possible, or at least to temper their sorrow and forget it for a while.

Thus Christ does not want to urge continual mourning and sorrow. He wants to warn against those who seek to escape all mourning and to have nothing but fun and all their comfort here. And He wants to teach His Christians, when things go badly for them and they have to mourn, to know that it is God's good pleasure and to make it theirs as well, not to curse or rage or despair as though their God did not want to be gracious. When this happens, the bitter draft should be mixed and made milder with honey and sugar. He promises here that this is pleasing to Him; and He calls them "blessed," comforting them here, and hereafter taking the sorrow away from them completely. Therefore say good-by to the world and to all those who harm us, in the name of their lord, the devil. And let us sing this song and be joyful in the name of God and Christ. Their outcome will surely not be the one they want. Now they take pleasure in our misfortune and do much to harm us. Still we take heart, and we shall live to see that at the last they will have to howl and weep when we are comforted and happy.

Blessed are the meek, for they shall inherit the earth. (Matthew 5:5)

This statement fits the first one well, when He said: "Blessed are the spiritually poor." For as He promises the kingdom of heaven and an eternal possession there, so here He also adds a promise about this temporal life and about possessions here on earth. But how does being poor harmonize with inheriting the land? It might seem that the preacher has forgotten how He began. Whoever is to inherit land and possessions cannot be poor. By "inheriting the land" here and having all sorts of possessions here on earth, He does not mean that everyone is to inherit a whole country; otherwise God would have to create more worlds. But God confers possessions upon everyone in such a way that He gives a man wife, children, cattle, house, and home, and whatever pertains to these, so that he can stay on the land where he lives and have dominion over his possessions. This is the way Scripture customarily speaks, as Psalm 37 says several times (Ps. 37:34): "Those who wait for the Lord will inherit the land"; and again (Ps. 37:22): "His blessed ones inherit the land." Therefore He adds His own gloss here: to be "spiritually poor," as He used the expression before, does not mean to be a beggar or to discard money and possessions. For here He tells them to live and remain in the land and to manage earthly possessions. . . .

What does it mean, then, to be meek? From the outset here you must realize that Christ is not speaking at all about the government and its work, whose property it is not to be meek, as we use the word in German, but to bear the sword (Rom. 13:4) for the punishment of those who do wrong (1 Peter 2:14), and to wreak a vengeance and a wrath that are called the vengeance and wrath of God. He is only talking about how individuals are to live in relation to others, apart from official position and authority—how father and mother are to live, not in relation to their children nor in their official capacity as father and mother, but in relation to those for whom they are not father and mother, like neighbors and other people. I have often said that we must sharply distinguish between these two, the office and the person. The man who is called Hans or Martin is a man quite different from the one who is called elector or doctor or preacher. Here we have two different persons in one man. The one is that in which we are created and born, according to which we are all alike—man or woman or child, young or old. But once we are born, God adorns and dresses you up as another person. He makes you a child and me a father, one a master and another a servant, one a prince and another a citizen. Then this one is called a divine person, one who holds a divine office and goes about clothed in its dignity—not simply Hans or Nick, but the Prince of Saxony, father, or master. He is not talking about this person here, letting it alone in its own office and rule, as He has ordained it. He is talking merely about how each individual, natural person is to behave in relation to others. . . .

You see, then, that here Christ is rebuking those crazy saints who think that everyone is master of the whole world and is entitled to be delivered from all suffering, to roar and bluster and violently to defend his property. And He teaches us that whoever wants to rule and possess his property, his possessions, house, and home in peace, must be meek, so that he may overlook things and act reasonably, putting up with just as much as he possibly can. It is inevitable that your neighbor will sometimes do you injury or harm, either accidentally or maliciously. If he did it accidentally, you do not improve the situation by refusing or being unable to endure anything. If he did it maliciously, you only irritate him by your violent scratching and pounding; meanwhile he is laughing at you and enjoying the fact that he is baiting and troubling you, so that you still cannot have any peace or quietly enjoy what is yours.

So select one of the two, whichever you prefer: either to live in human society with meekness and patience and to hold on to what you have with peace and a good conscience; or boisterously and blusterously to lose what is yours, and to have no peace besides. There stands the decree: "The meek shall inherit the earth." Just take a look for yourself at the queer characters who are always arguing and squabbling about property and other things. They refuse to give in to anybody, but insist on rushing everything through headlong, regardless of whether their quarreling and squabbling costs them more than they could ever gain. Ultimately they lose their land and servants, house and home, and get unrest and a bad conscience thrown in. And God adds His blessing to it, saying: "Do not be meek, then, so that you may not keep your precious land, nor enjoy your morsel in peace."

But if you want to do right and have rest, let your neighbor's malice and viciousness smother and burn itself out. . . . Do you have a government? Then register a complaint, and let it see to it. The government has the charge not to permit the harsh oppression of the innocent. God will also overrule so that His Word and ordinance may abide and you may inherit the land according to this promise. Thus you will have rest and God's blessing, but your neighbor will have unrest together with God's displeasure and curse. This sermon is intended only for those who are Christians, who believe and know that they have their treasure in heaven, where it is secure for them and cannot be taken away: Hence they must have enough here, too, even though they do not have treasuries and pockets full of yellow guldens. Since you know this, why let your joy be disturbed and taken away? Why cause yourself disquiet and rob yourself of this magnificent promise?

See now that you have three points with three rich promises. Whoever is a Christian must have enough of both the temporal and the eternal, though here he must suffer much both outwardly and inwardly, in the heart. On the other hand, because the worldlings refuse to endure poverty or trouble or violence, they neither have the kingdom of heaven nor enjoy temporal goods peacefully and quietly. . . .

Marty: We are not trying to improve on the sources "Matthew" used or on the Gospel of Matthew by rearranging the sequence of chapters in the Sermon on the Mount. In the Bible the Beatitudes come before the words we have already discussed, words about anxiety and advice about prayer, climaxing in the Lord's Prayer. Here the words about being blessed follow those other two selections, and this for a specific reason: in our plot, the words about who is blessed will make most sense if we have become more clear about why we should not be anxious and why and how we should pray.

The Gospel spends little time giving the Sermon on the Mount a setting. A movie director like the one who filmed *Ben Hur* spends many hours or days finding the right kind of hill, clearing it of rocks, seeing to it that the grass on its slopes is green, and that a good crowd will be visible to the camera person. Here it is simply: "When Jesus saw the crowds, he went up the mountain; and after he sat down, his disciples came to him. Then he began to speak, and taught them, saying" (5:1-2, NRSV).

The film-makers, eager to provide spectacle, also crowd the scene, as if they were filming the Gospel accounts of Jesus feeding the 5,000, or, in another version, 4,000. Or they want viewers to picture that his circle of disciples has grown very large very early on. Not so, as the evangelist frames it. In your Bible, only two or three inches of print above the beginning of the Sermon on the Mount is the story of Jesus attracting disciples: Simon Peter, Andrew, James, and John get mentioned. He bade them come and they "followed him." Matthew does not get called and mentioned until after the Sermon, in chapter nine.

Still, as this Gospel tells it, word must have traveled fast, because more than the named persons, more than the twelve were present. "The crowds were astonished at his teaching." The Gospel writers are deliciously imprecise. They want to convey two ideas: that disciples as insiders need special instruction, and these words, we are told, were spoken to them just as they are written for us. And these words are compelling, so the circle of those who hear them, ponder them, and tell about them grows. Simply, "he taught them, saying. . . ."

And in Matthew he was saying what we call The Beatitudes. "Beatitudes" is a word we never have to learn or use apart from the Sermon on the Mount. It is not even in the Bible. Greek scholars have their own word for the literary form used here: "macarisms," which builds on the Greek word for blessing (*makarios*). In our culture we cannot take for granted that the word for even this most favored set of biblical quotations is familiar. I once heard a disk jockey refer to them as "The Beautitudes" (as in "beautiful"). No one called in to correct him, and a half hour later he repeated the mispronunciation. Maybe he had something: there is beauty in these blessings, even if most of them have a downside: if the ones the text mentions are blessed, what about the great majority of the unmentioned, unblessed?

We hear Jesus turning first to the "spiritually poor," for "theirs is the kingdom of heaven." If what we said earlier about the kingdom is valid—that it refers to the saving activity of a sovereign God—we picture the spiritually poor as swept up in it. Earth offers little, but the kingdom means "being saved." That means being named by God, identified with Jesus Christ, rescued from whatever holds them back from God. It does not mean that they will be rich, have a good job, have people bowing as they walk by or being impressed by their resumé. Let's listen to Luther as he converses with this text about the "spiritually poor."

He is almost ecstatic about what he reads. As far as he is concerned, these "Blessed are . . ." phrases are the first words a reader of the Bible "hears" from Jesus. Scholars today tend to think that Mark is older. In that case the first words would have sounded an alarm, being a bit more confrontational, demanding decision: "The time is fulfilled, and the kingdom of God has come near; repent and believe in the good news" (Mark 1:14-15, NRSV).

So it is "Repent!" versus "Blessed are . . .". Those of us who have known the joy of repenting and then being forgiven know what "blessed" means, and Jesus could not have included the unrepentant among the "spiritually poor." These are different accents. Luther likes the Matthew version. Jesus is not someone who demands, threatens, or terrifies; but rather he entices, lures, and promises. Luther pictures that if we had some notion of who Jesus was and is, and what he was and is about, but did not have these recorded words, we would all race to Jerusalem, or further, to hear one single word of it. Foundations, philanthropic organizations, stewardship committees, and taxing agencies would have no trouble coming up with road-building funds to help us get there. And whoever got there would have bragging rights: "I heard the first word Jesus said, and it was 'Blessed. . . .'" Those who did hear of Jesus through St. Paul would still want to hear something direct from Jesus. And, directly, Jesus blesses.

Luther knows what habit can do to dim excitement. What once startled, shocked, or inspired gets to be familiar and we lose our curiosity to hear it, or our ability to let it soak in. So we get little out of it. He invites us, in effect, to forget we ever heard it before, and listen. Nothing in what he said matches what we find on the financial pages of our newspapers, what we put into college curricula to help graduates outpace their classmates, in the way we organize our finances, or what we invest in. In these words we learn that Jesus upsets the way we usually think about things. Some teachers will say that we can never understand a parable or a saying of Jesus until we learn that he is always out to jostle us and overturn our usual way of looking at things.

He does so here. He opens his mouth, Luther says, and out comes a blessing that is a call for us to shift priorities. If he were commenting as recently as yesterday, he could not be more discerning or relevant about our situation than he is when he puts into Jesus' mind and on his tongue some words that reflect how we think, not how God is revealed. He takes a quick swipe at Jews for thinking that success was a sign of God's favor, "and vice versa." But we all know that you did not have to be a Jew, and don't need to be now, to connect success with grace or grace with success and material rewards.

For a moment Luther is charitable and bids us to have a second look. There were, in his eyes, good reason for people to think that such favoring went on, because God was generous in giving promises and fulfilling them. When they have setbacks, in such reasoning, they must have done something wrong. It is easy to find such scary pop theology today. So you lost health or a dear one or some assets or opportunities? Then you have to ask what you did to anger God into action against you. Not in the world that Luther learned from the biblical book of Job and that he here passes on to us.

Job had to purge the delusions of his friends, who connected success and the action of a loving God. He had to tear them out of the heart. If we live by that delusion, we will be greedy epicureans. We would also look around and determine who must have pleased God by noticing who looked blessed or deprived. If we think that way, we are not alone: "This is still what the whole world believes today" in this "most universal belief or religion on earth." That is why Jesus has to jolt believers in that religious commitment, or they will never be "blessed."

In a conversation in which one represents the many, he or she has to imagine what the many are thinking. Luther thinks that "we" think that he is saying we dare not have "money, property, popularity, power, and the like" if we want to be swept up by the kingdom. But, no! He does not let us think that the gaining or abandoning of property by itself as being the ticket to or the barrier against the kingdom. He moves us to the little adverb "spiritually" smuggled in next to "poor," from the simply secular longing for stuff. What is at issue is the location of the object of our trust. Placing confidence, seeking comfort, locating trust in temporal objects, makes Mammon God, and God is not God in the hearts of those who get this mixed up.

While we like to have a place called home, where we can unpack and settle in, Luther says that in respect to the kingdom of heaven we can forget about owning, possessing, hoarding, or piling up. Think "temporary." Think "guest." He hears Jesus saying that we should use all goods and necessities the way we do when we are overnight guests who leave in the morning. Say, "This is mine, here I will stay," and you may be unceremoniously moved on with a reminder that this is not yours. At night and in the morning the host's possessions are to be of use, but they do not become the property of the guest.

Just as here the Sermon on the Mount speaks of the spiritually poor, Luther reminds us that the words of Jesus also speak of the "rich bellies," who own much but are never satisfied and who never seek the blessing of God. In these paragraphs and elsewhere, what matters is the character of the heart, not the marks of wealth or poverty. No one should desert home and possessions, as if doing so by itself will assure the kingdom of heaven. Everyone should learn not to get attached to what they temporarily possess. God has God's own way of setting time and sending out messages.

As if supposing that we have gotten that point, our commentator turns attention to the rest of the verse: "For of such is the kingdom of heaven." Here Luther says that the kingdom of heaven will be in heaven, beyond earthly systems of rewards and punishment. Abruptly: "This sermon does the world no good and accomplishes nothing for it." Such a notion dooms all those self-help books that tell how to get rich if you follow the words of Jesus in the Bible. Christ does not browbeat us into acceptance of his way; he extends it as an option, and we are free to follow, or not. "If you do not want it, have your own way. . . ." That's a bad choice. All this is a word against greed and grasping, and for acceptance and use of what God gives.

Here comes Overturning Number Two: "Blessed are those who mourn, for they shall be comforted" (5:4). Here it is important to notice that Jesus is not commanding that we should mourn. Luther the psychologist has observed too many people who thought they could please God by having the grumps, being down in the mouth, garbed in black veils, and encouraging tears to flow. No one, we read, can stand continual mourning. "It sucks out the very strength and savor of the body." Saying that and doing something about it are too different things. We know too much about the biography of Martin Luther to be so naïve as to think that he learned his own lesson. He could get depressed, sulk, grieve, mourn, and hang his head so effectively that we are told his wife Katherine once had to come to him dressed in black. She evidently "overturned" his thinking enough that he looked up and asked what happened. This story goes on to say that she told him God must have died, since all of Martin's appearance suggested just that.

As we read lines of comment like these, it is important to realize that mourning can have many sources. Neuron firings in the brain may be off a bit, and chemical reactions can go wrong, so we are depressed. Luther could not have known much about how one fights off the tendency to mourn disproportionately to the circumstances, but he does have some therapy when it comes, counsel that he himself sometimes took, as when he puts into print what he surmises we are thinking: "Is everyone to be damned who laughs, sings, dances, dresses well, eats, and drinks," and has not taken mourning lessons from the professionals? Over against this he calls on the apostle Paul and hears him saying that we are to be cheerful all the time. I hope this does not mean that we have to paste a smile on, and can never cry. It evidently means that we are not to be given over to mourning, as if the God of promise is not present, or could not deliver.

If "being spiritually poor" was a matter of the heart, not of possessions; now being blessed as a mourner means that we do not have to lapse into deep and permanent gloom. Of course, tears well up in us when we lose a loved one, and not to mourn them would be unnatural and a kind of desecration. But enough is enough, we hear here. Excessive and unrelieved mourning does no good for the mourned, the mourner, or those who suffer from the mourner's commitment to being gloomy.

Avoiding what licenses or forces mourning—"enduring hunger, trouble, dishonor, unpopularity, injustice, and violence"—comes naturally, but all of these troubles will come, unbidden, often unannounced. Luther is here defining negative from positive mourning. Jesus is heard blessing mourners not because they are virtuosos at grieving but because really bad things really do come, and those who endure and turn in faith to the God of comfort will realize comfort.

More counsel: you cannot avoid bad things that evoke mourning. Bad things happen, and the mere fact of their happening is bad enough. It is worse when someone goes looking for them, having adopted the style of the permanent mourner. Just becoming a Christian will give a believer enough to be sad about. Yes, you read it here, citing the same Luther who says that we have reasons for cheer, are always to hope, never to be profoundly depressed. But he does not linger long on the mere sadness, the occasions for mourning. In fact, very quickly he talks about how those who mourn in faith "are entitled to have fun and to take it wherever they can so that they do not completely collapse for sorrow." Just don't count on nothing but fun. Count on God's grace and presence not to desert you.

One more overturning and upsetting in respect to the way we naturally think follows those about the spiritually pure and the mourners: "Blessed are the meek, for they shall inherit the earth" (5:5).

Here, at least as much as in the other two cases, the word of the Sermon on the Mount goes against the culture we inhabit. Blessed are the meek? The meek get caricatured. We have met them in movies, plays, television dramas, and books. Jesus might as well have said "Blessed are the nerds" or "Blessed are the wimps" or " Blessed are those who say 'Pardon me' and mean it, who say 'After you,' and let you to go through the turnstile first."

It would have been easier had Jesus not jostled us with such overturning. He could have said "Blessed are the macho types" or "Blessed are those who can shout 'We're Number One.'" If he thought as the world thinks instead of as the one he calls Father thinks, he would have made it easier for us to live in an "in-your-face" culture, where swaggering and gloating fit. For a moment off camera you may hear an admiring word for the humble and even the meek, but when the lights come on or the headline writers and advertisers get ready, it is the proud and the bold who look like the blessed.

Luther listens carefully and, placing himself at our side, has heard and reports on something plaguing. Jesus had blessed the spiritually poor and now he gives the promise that the meek shall "inherit the earth." How, he asks, can someone inherit the land and possessions and still be poor? These two blesseds seem to contradict each other, even cancel each other out. Luther almost sounds irreverent as he poses this apparent contradiction: "But how does being poor harmonize with inheriting the land? It might seem that the preacher has forgotten how He began." He softens his answer by going back to Scripture and reading promises to individuals that they will possess some land and may own a house. And he ties that to stewardship: God gives enough that those who take care can have a measure of possessions. Don't be a beggar and throw away possessions. Earthly possessions find their place if the heart is right.

So we have to deal with "the meek."

The government cannot be meek, we read, because it must punish. (Since wreaking wrath and vengeance is by no means the only work of government, I could wish he might have introduced ways in which those who govern could be not meek but also not vengeance-bound. But that is another topic for another day.) Here the whole stress is on the individual, a member of the group that become "the meek" in the Matthew passage.

The commentator turns schoolmasterly here and goes into more detail. Once more he teaches the difference between an "office" and a "person." All are created as persons, and God places each into some situation, circumstance, or position that here gets called office. One might have to be other than meek outside of the "office" but must always be meek as the person. One can think of Hans or Nick off-stage or backstage, and Hans and Nick are supposed to be meek, while onstage he may be "the Prince of Saxony" in a nonmeek role.

That distinction probably does not solve as much as Luther would like it to, but he moves on to a point that speaks to the day. The individual who as individual wants to rule and possess his property has to be meek, which means to be able to overlook some things and be reasonable in action, "putting up with just as much as he possibly can." If a neighbor treats you badly and does so accidentally, be meek in responding. If he did it maliciously, be meek in responding. Act in ways opposite to "meek" and you will have him taking revenge, heating things up. Which do you prefer? we get asked. Squabblers and arguers waste energy, fire up rivals, and lose everything while gaining a bad conscience. That's no bargain. All of this advice about the negative side of things is practical and good, though hard to follow and not always connected, I suppose, to what the line about the meek inheriting the earth is saying.

We turn the page on this one, not necessarily satisfied by what its predecessor pages say about how governments act justly and should be left alone, but spurred to what is ahead because the advice to individuals seems well-directed and helpful.

For reflection

1. Comment on the surprising, overturning nature of the Beatitudes discussed in this chapter. How do these statements of blessing seem to hold up or "fit" in today's world?

2. What does it mean to be "spiritually poor"? How does it help to think of our time here on earth as guest?

3. Mourning is not to be worn like a badge of honor or sought out as the Christian's way of being—just so we might earn a blessing. So, when are the mournful blessed?

4. How does the call to "be meek" in 5:5 seem at odds with "worldly" thinking? How can one be meek enough to inherit the world without getting brushed aside as weak or irrelevant?

5. What new learning or insight do you take from this chapter? How has your faith and sense of trust been strengthened?

7

Hungering for Justice

Blessed are those who hunger and thirst for righteousness, for they shall be satisfied.

⇄ *Matthew 5:6*

Luther: "Righteousness" in this passage must not be taken in the sense of that principal Christian righteousness by which a person becomes pious and acceptable to God. I have said before that these eight items are nothing but instruction about the fruits and good works of a Christian. Before these must come faith, as the tree and chief part or summary of a man's righteousness and blessedness, without any work or merit of his; out of which faith these items all must grow and follow. Therefore take this in the sense of the outward righteousness before the world, which we maintain in our relations with each other. Thus the short and simple meaning of these words is this: "That man is righteous and blessed who continually works and strives with all his might to promote the general welfare and the proper behavior of everyone and who helps to maintain and support this by word and deed, by precept and example."

Now, this is also a precious point, embracing very many good works, but by no means a common thing. Let me illustrate with an example. If a preacher wants to qualify under this point, he must be ready to instruct and help everyone to perform his assigned task properly and to do what it requires. And when he sees that something is missing and things are not going right, he should be on hand to warn, rebuke, and correct by whatever method or means he can. Thus as a preacher I dare not neglect my office. Nor dare the others neglect theirs, which is, to follow my teaching and preaching. In this way the right thing is done on both sides. Now, where there are people who earnestly take it upon themselves to do right gladly and to be found engaged in the right works and ways—such people "hunger and thirst for righteousness." If this were the situation, there would be no rascality or injustice, but sheer righteousness and blessedness on earth. What is the righteousness of the world except that in his station everyone should do his duty? That means that the rights of every station should be respected—those of the man, the woman, the child, the manservant, and the maid in the household, the citizen of the city in the land. And it is all contained in this, that those who are charged with overseeing and ruling other people should execute this office diligently, carefully, and faithfully, and that the others should also render their due service and obedience to them faithfully and willingly.

It is not by accident that He uses the term "hunger and thirst for righteousness." By it He intends to point out that this requires great earnestness, longing, eagerness, and unceasing diligence and that where this hunger and thirst is lacking, everything will fail. The reason is that there are too many great hindrances. They come from the devil, who is blocking and barricading the way everywhere. They also come from the world—that is, his children—which is so wicked that it cannot stand a pious man who wants to do right himself or to help other people do so, but plagues him in every way, that he finally becomes tired and perplexed over the whole business. It is painful to see how shamefully people behave, and to get no reward for pure kindness except ingratitude, contempt, hate, and persecution. For this reason, many people who could not stand the sight of such evil conduct finally despaired over it, ran away from human society into the desert, and became monks, so that the saying has repeatedly been verified: "Despair makes a man a monk." A person may not trust himself to make his own living and run into the monastery for his belly's sake, as the great crowd has done; otherwise a person may despair of the world and not trust himself in it, either to remain pious or to help people.

But this is not hungering and thirsting for righteousness. Anyone who tries to preach or rule in such a way that he lets himself become tired and impatient and be chased into a corner will not be of much help to other people. The command to you is not to crawl into a corner or into the desert, but to run out, if that is where you have been, and to offer your hands and your feet and your whole body, and to wager everything you have and can do. You should be the kind of man who is firm in the face of firmness, who will not let himself be frightened off or dumbfounded or overcome by the world's ingratitude or malice, who will always hold on and push with all the might he can summon. In short, the ministry requires a hunger and thirst for righteousness that can never be curbed or stopped or sated, one that looks for nothing and cares for nothing except the accomplishment and maintenance of the right, despising everything that hinders this end. If you cannot make the world completely pious, then do what you can. It is enough that you have done your duty and have helped a few, even if there be only one or two. If others will not follow, then in God's name let them go. You must not run away on account of the wicked, but rather conclude: "I did not undertake this for their sakes, and I shall not drop it for their sakes. Eventually some of them might come around; at least there might be fewer of them, and they may improve a little."

Here you have a comforting and certain promise, with which Christ allures and attracts His Christians: "Those who hunger and thirst for righteousness shall be filled." That is, they will be recompensed for their hunger and thirst by seeing that their work was not in vain and that at last a little flock has been brought around who have been helped. Although things are not going now as they would like and they have almost despaired over it, all this will become manifest, not only here on earth, but even more in the life hereafter, when everyone will see what sort of fruit such people have brought by their diligence and perseverance. For example, a pious preacher has snatched many souls out of the jaws of the devil and brought them to heaven; or a pious, faithful ruler has helped many lands and people, who testify that he has done so and who praise him before the whole world.

The counterfeit saints are exactly the opposite. Because of their great sanctity they forsake the world and run into the desert, or they sneak away into a corner somewhere, to escape the trouble and worry that they would otherwise have to bear. They do not want to pay attention to what is going on in the world. Never once do they think of the fact that they should help or advise other people with teaching, instruction, warning, reproof, correction, or at least with prayers and sighs to God. Yes, it even disgusts and grieves them when other people become pious; for they want to be thought of as the only ones who are holy so that anyone who wants to get to heaven has to buy their good works and merits from them. In brief, they are so full of righteousness that they look down their noses at other poor sinners. Just so in Luke 18:11 the great St. Pharisee in his intoxication looks down at the poor publican and spits on him. He is so much in love with himself that he pays court to God and thanks Him that he alone is pious and other people are bad.

Note that these are the people against whom Christ is speaking here, the shameful, proud, and self-sufficient spirits, who are tickled, pleased, and overjoyed over the fact that other people are not pious, whereas they ought to pity them, sympathize with them, and help them. All they can do is to despise, slander, judge, and condemn everyone else; everything must be stench and filth except what they themselves do. But going out to admonish and help a poor, frail sinner—this they avoid as they would avoid the devil. Hence they will have to hear again what Christ cries out against them in Luke 6:25: "Woe to you that are full, for you shall hunger." As those who now hunger and thirst shall be filled, so these others must hunger forever; though they are full and sated now, no one has ever got any benefit from them or been able to praise them for ever helping anyone or setting him aright. There you have a summary of the meaning of this passage, which, as I have said, embraces many good works, indeed, all the good works by which a man may live right by himself in human society and help to give success to all sorts of offices and stations, as I have often said in more detail elsewhere.

Blessed are the merciful, for they shall obtain mercy. (5:7)

This is also an outstanding fruit of faith, and it follows well upon what went before. Anyone who is supposed to help other people and to contribute to the common weal and success should also be kind and merciful. He should not immediately raise a rumpus and start a riot if something is missing or if things do not go as they should, as long as there is still some hope for improvement. One of the virtues of counterfeit sanctity is that it cannot have pity or mercy for the frail and weak, but insists on the strictest enforcement and the purest selection; as soon as there is even a minor flaw, all mercy is gone, and there is nothing but fuming and fury. St. Gregory also teaches us how to recognize this when he says: "True justice shows mercy, but false justice shows indignation." True holiness is merciful and sympathetic, but all that false holiness can do is to rage and fume. Yet it does so, as they boast, "out of zeal for justice"; that is, it is done through love and zeal for righteousness.

The whole world is being forced to the conclusion that they have been carrying on their mischief and violence under the lovely and excellent pretext and cover of doing it for the sake of righteousness. In the same way, both in the past and in the present, they have been exercising their enmity and treachery against the Gospel under the guise of defending the truth and exterminating heresy. For this they want God to crown them and to elevate them to heaven, as a reward for those who out of great thirst and hunger for righteousness persecute, strangle, and burn His saints.

They want to make the claim and to give the impression, even more than the true saints, that they hunger and thirst for righteousness. They put up such a good front and use such beautiful words that they think even God Himself will not know any better. But the noble tree is known by its fruits. When they should demand justice, that is, the proper administration of both the spiritual and the temporal realm, they do not do so. It never enters their mind to instruct and improve anyone. They themselves live in continual vice; and if anyone denounces their behavior or does not praise it and do as they want, he must be a heretic and let himself be damned to hell. You see, that is how it is with every counterfeit saint. His self-made holiness makes him so proud that he despises everyone else and cannot have a kind and merciful heart.

Therefore this is a necessary warning against such abominable saints. If a man deals with his neighbor in an effort to help and correct him in his station and way of life, he should still take care to be merciful and to forgive. In this way people will see that your aim really is righteousness and not the gratification of your own malice and anger; for you are righteous enough to deal in a friendly and gentle manner with the man who is willing to forsake his unrighteousness and improve himself, and you tolerate and endure his fault or weakness until he comes around. But if you try all this and find no hope for improvement, then you may give him up and turn him over to those whose duty it is to punish.

Now, this is the one aspect of mercy, that one gladly forgives the sinful and the frail. The other is to do good also to those who are outwardly poor or in need of help; on the basis of Matthew 25:35 ff. we call these "works of mercy." The arrogant Jewish saints knew nothing about this aspect either. There was nothing in them but ice and frost—yes, a heart as hard as a block of stone—and not a single loving drop of blood that took pleasure in doing good for a neighbor, nor any mercy that forgave sin. All they were concerned about and thought about was their own belly, even though another man might have been starving to death. Thus there is much more mercy among public sinners than there is in such a saint. This is how it has to be; for they praise only themselves and regard only themselves as holy, despising everyone else as worthless and supposing that the whole world must serve them and give them plenty, while they are under no obligation to give anyone anything or any service.

Hence this sermon and exhortation seems contemptible and useless to such saints. The only pupils it finds are those who already cling to Christ and believe in Him. They know of no holiness of their own. On the basis of the preceding items they are poor, miserable, meek, really hungry and thirsty; they are inclined not to despise anyone, but to assume and to sympathize with the need of everyone else. To them applies the comforting promise: "It is well with you who are merciful. For you will find pure mercy in turn, both here and hereafter, and a mercy which inexpressibly surpasses all human kindness and mercy." There is no comparison between our mercy and God's, nor between our possessions and the eternal possessions in the kingdom of heaven. So pleased is He with our kindness to our neighbor that for one pfennig He promises us a hundred thousand guldens if we have need of them, and for a drink of water, the kingdom of heaven (Matt. 10:42).

Now, if anyone will not let himself be moved by this wonderful and comforting promise, let him turn the page and hear another judgment: "Woe and curses upon the unmerciful, for no mercy shall be shown to them." At the present time the world is full of people, among the nobles and city people and peasants, who sin very grievously against the dear Gospel. Not only do they refuse to give support or help to poor ministers and preachers; but besides they commit theft and torment against it wherever they can, and act as if they meant to starve it out and chase it out of the world. Meanwhile they go along quite smugly, supposing that God must keep quiet about it and approve of everything they do. But it will hit them someday. I am afraid that someone will come along who will make a prophet out of me—for I have given ample warning—and treat them mercilessly, taking away their reputation and their property, their body and their life, so that the Word of God might remain true and so that he who refuses to show or to have mercy might experience endless wrath and eternal displeasure. As St. James also says (James 2:13): "Judgment without mercy will be spoken over the one who has shown no mercy." At the Last Day, therefore, Christ will also cite this lack of mercy as the worst injury done to Him, whatever we have done out of a lack of mercy. He Himself will utter the curse (Matt. 25:41, 42): "I was hungry and thirsty, and you gave me no food, you gave me no drink. Depart from me, therefore, you cursed, into eternal hell-fire." He warns and exhorts us faithfully, out of sheer grace and mercy. Whoever does not want to accept this, let him choose the curse and eternal damnation. Think of the rich man in Luke 16; daily he saw poor Lazarus lying before his door full of sores, yet he did not have enough mercy to give him a bundle of straw or to grant him the crumbs under his table. But look how terribly he was requited; in hell he would gladly have given a hundred thousand guldens for the privilege of boasting that he had given him even a thread.

Marty: It would be easy to read the first three of the Beatitudes as addresses to our selfish needs. We don't like to be poor, would rather not have to mourn, and would like to inherit something or other of the earth. So it is good to be promised the kingdom, comfort, and goods, though in every case we may by now have found that each of these terms has a special meaning in the light of the activity of God.

The next set of people, however, look outward: "Blessed are those who hunger and thirst for righteousness, for they will be filled." Hungering for righteousness means a desire to set the world aright, to work for justice for ourselves but, better, justice for more, for all. To wake up this morning and think of not being poor, of rejoicing, of gaining is quite natural. Unless the first thought is of an injustice being worked out against us—and, admit it, one often is—we are less likely to put this item at the center of the agenda.

The first radio or television program of the day, the newspaper tossed on the porch, the weekly magazine waiting next to breakfast coffee, all these are full of stories about a world in which righteousness and justice are lacking. We ought to do something about these. Many of us will have opportunities as the day goes on to do so. The teacher who finds ways to deter a bully is doing his part. The executive who addresses issues of unfair labor practices may be doing hers. A legislator or a judge can hunger for and help produce some measure of right judgment and fairness. But we may also resign ourselves to the world in which injustice outweighs justice, evil overburdens the scales where righteousness should be most weighty. Wherever we locate the hunger and thirst for righteousness on our agenda, the Jesus of the Sermon on the Mount places them up among the most desired and needed things imaginable.

Whoever knows him well knows that another lesson is coming away from Professor Luther whenever the word "righteousness" shows up. Here it comes: he says the righteousness here spoken of is not of the sort that makes one right with God, the sort on the basis of which God acts to declare the sinner righteous. He makes a distinction between the righteousness that avails before God, which is always and only through the gift of God in Jesus Christ on one hand, and, on the other, righteousness in the sense of just actions among humans.

Begin with the tree before you talk about good or bad fruits, says Luther. The tree is faith, the chief part of a person's righteousness. Then can follow what he calls "outward righteousness before the world," which means having right relations with other humans. I don't know where Luther got his definition of the righteous person, but I picture him making it up and, as we say in the world of computers, "pasting it in" to the commentary. While you have just read it in the passage of Luther on which I am commenting, I find it useful to repeat it here:

"That man is righteous and blessed who continually works and strives with all his might to promote the general welfare and the proper behavior of everyone and who helps to maintain and support this by word and deed, by precept and example." "Promote the general welfare" is a good theme about government in the United States, as well as about citizen action. The word "continually" is also important. You don't hunger or thirst for righteousness as a part-timer, a Sunday soldier, but rather as someone who, while having a job and a life to live, is always also on duty on this front.

If people pursued righteousness, they would leave behind rascality or injustice, simply by doing their duty as citizens, and would live responsibly. Luther likes it that Jesus used bodily terms to describe how to find and appraise responsible people. They "hunger and thirst." The pursuit is demanding, blocked at so many places, often unrewarded, sometimes advanced. But, at least to my slight disappointment, he lets this Beatitude speak mainly to people in government and law enforcement, in a world so different from our own that it is more efficient to track down biblical teaching on this subject elsewhere.

Still, we cannot leave it without paying some attention to the promise that those zealous for food and drink "shall be filled." They will get their reward in the life hereafter, when the people they have helped by being just and acting justly will recognize the benefit, the fruit that the righteous governing person cultivates. For the rest, let it be a little lesson in 16th century governmental life, and we are staying with 21st century possibilities. We wish well to those who seek righteousness, Luther's model, and get encouraged when we see a passion for justice rewarded so the further spread of justice can occur.

In the Bible, justice usually gets paired with mercy. Here the link is perfect after the noisier talk about mercy in the public realm, in the governmental order. This quiet word is welcome: the merciful shall obtain mercy. Governments are not expected to be meek and get along with the task of serving well if they are. They and all people in authority are expected to be merciful. If things do not work out, they are not to cause a riot in compensatory fury. Luther quotes St. Gregory: "True justice shows mercy, but false justice shows indignation." It is easy to claim that one is passionate about justice, and show rage while wreaking vengeance. It is harder to be and remain compassionate and thus merciful in public life.

Showing mercy is even practical and prudential. People will discern that someone who rules or governs is not acting out of malice or anger but out of love. So much does Luther dwell on what righteousness means in public life that one almost forgets to watch for his comment in a realm in which he was more at ease. Show mercy in private life and people will trust you, because they understand that you are not working off your temper but showing an example of forgiveness. In fact, while he gives only a few lines to the subject, Luther reserves his own scorn for those who judge but show no mercy, since they fail to find Christ in the person pleading for mercy from humans.

For reflection

1. When Luther speaks of righteousness, he speaks of it in two ways. What two meanings of this word are at play in his comments? How do the two concepts "survive" together, or better, "complement one another"?

2. Have you ever known someone who seemed to hunger or thirst for righteousness? Describe that person. What "blessing" did they seem to derive from this thirst, and what blessings did they pass on to others?

3. What does it mean to show mercy to another person? Has anyone ever been merciful toward you. Describe the situation. In what way is showing mercy like, or perhaps unlike, forgiving someone?

4. What new insight have you discovered in this chapter?

8

Pure-hearted Peacemakers

Blessed are the pure in heart, for they shall see God.

☘ *Matthew 5:8*

Luther: What is meant by a "pure heart" is this: one that is watching and pondering what God says and replacing its own ideas with the Word of God. This alone is pure before God, yes, purity itself, which purifies everything that it includes and touches. Therefore, though a common laborer, a shoemaker, or a blacksmith may be dirty and sooty or may smell because he is covered with dirt and pitch, still he may sit at home and think: "My God has made me a man. He has given me my house, wife, and child and has commanded me to love them and to support them with my work." Note that he is pondering the Word of God in his heart; and though he stinks outwardly, inwardly he is pure incense before God. But if he attains the highest purity so that he also takes hold of the Gospel and believes in Christ—without this, that purity is impossible—then he is pure completely, inwardly in his heart toward God and outwardly toward everything under him on earth. Then everything he is and does, his walking, standing, eating, and drinking, is pure for him; and nothing can make him impure. So it is when he looks at his own wife or fondles her, as the patriarch Isaac did (Gen. 26:8), which a monk regards as disgusting and defiling. For here he has the Word of God, and he knows that God has given her to him. But if he were to desert his wife and take up another, or neglect his job or duty to harm or bother other people, he would no longer be pure; for that would be contrary to God's commandment.

But so long as he sticks to these two—namely, the Word of faith toward God, which purifies the heart, and the Word of Understanding, which teaches him what he is to do toward his neighbor . . . —everything is pure for him, even if with his hands and the rest of his body he handles nothing but dirt. If a poor housemaid does her duty and is a Christian in addition, then before God in heaven she is a lovely and pure beauty, one that all the angels admire and love to look at. . . .

So you see that everything depends on the Word of God. Whatever is included in that and goes in accordance with it, must be called clean, pure, and white as snow before both God and man. Therefore Paul says (Titus 1:15): "To the pure all things are pure"; and again: "To the corrupt and unbelieving nothing is pure." Why is this so? Because both their minds and their consciences are impure. How does this happen? Because "they profess to know God, but with their deeds they deny it" (Titus 1:16). . . .

. . . Whatever God does and ordains must be pure and good. For He makes nothing impure, and He consecrates everything through the Word which He has attached to every station and creature.

Therefore be on guard against all your own ideas if you want to be pure before God. See to it that your heart is founded and fastened on the Word of God. Then you will be purer than all the Carthusians and saints in the world. When I was young, people used to take pride in this proverb: "Enjoy being alone, and your heart will stay pure." In support of it they would cite a quotation from St. Bernard, who said that whenever he was among people, he defiled himself. In the lives of the fathers we read about a hermit who would not let anyone come near him or talk to him, because, he said: "The angels cannot come to anyone who moves around in human society." We also read about two others, who would not let their mother see them. She kept watch, and once she caught them. Immediately they closed the door and let her stand outside for a long time crying; finally they persuaded her to go away and to wait until they would see each other in the life hereafter. . . .

(Instead of seeking pureness through such a solitary life, let it be) where God has put it, in a heart that clings to God's Word and that regards its tasks and every creature on the basis of it. Then the chief purity, that of faith toward God, will also manifest itself outwardly in this life; and everything will proceed from obedience to the Word and command of God, regardless of whether it is physically clean or unclean. I spoke earlier of a judge who has to condemn a man to death, who thus sheds blood and defiles himself with it. A monk would regard this as an abominably impure act, but Scripture says it is the service of God. In Rom. 13:4 Paul calls the government, which bears the sword, "God's servant." This is not its work and command, but His, which He imposes on it and demands from it.

Now you have the meaning of "pure heart": it is one that functions completely on the basis of the pure Word of God. What is their reward, what does He promise to them? It is this: "They shall see God." A wonderful title and an excellent treasure! But what does it mean to "see God"? Here again the monks have their own dreams. To them it means sitting in a cell and elevating your thoughts heavenward, leading a "contemplative life," as they call it in the many books they have written about it. . . . But this is what it is: if you have a true faith that Christ is your Savior, then you see immediately that you have a gracious God. For faith leads you up and opens up the heart and will of God for you. There you see sheer, superabundant grace and love. That is exactly what it means "to see God," not with physical eyes, with which no one can see Him in this life, but with faith, which sees His fatherly, friendly heart, where there is no anger or displeasure. Anyone who regards Him as angry is not seeing Him correctly, but has pulled down a curtain and cover, more, a dark cloud over His face. But in Scriptural language "to see His face" means to recognize Him correctly as a gracious and faithful Father, on whom you can depend for every good thing. This happens only through faith in Christ.

Therefore, if according to God's Word and command you live in your station with your husband, wife, child, neighbor, or friend, you can see God's intention in these things; and you can come to the conclusion that they please Him, since this is not your own dream, but His Word and command, which never deludes or deceives us. It is a wonderful thing, a treasure beyond every thought or wish, to know that you are standing and living in the right relation to God. In this way not only can your heart take comfort and pride in the assurance of His grace, but you can know that your outward conduct and behavior is pleasing to Him. From this it follows that cheerfully and heartily you can do and suffer anything, without letting it make you fearful or despondent. None of this is possible for those who lack this faith and pure heart, guided only by God's Word. . . .

. . . No one can boast that in all his life and activity he has ever seen God. Or if in his pride someone glorifies such works and thinks that God must be well disposed to them and reward him for them, he is not seeing God but the devil in place of God. There is no word of God to support him; it is all the invention of men, grown up in their own hearts. That is why it can never assure or pacify any heart, but remain hidden by pride until it comes to its final gasps, when it all disappears and brings on despair, so that one never gets around to seeing the face of God. But anyone who takes hold of the Word of God and who remains in faith can take his stand before God and look at Him as his gracious Father. He does not have to be afraid that He is standing behind him with a club, and he is sure that He is looking at him and smiling graciously, together with all the angels and saints in heaven.

You see, that is what Christ means by this statement, that only those who have such a pure heart see God. By this He cuts off and puts aside every other kind of purity. Where this kind is absent, everything else in a man may be pure; but it is worth nothing before God, and he can never see God. Where the heart is pure, on the other hand, everything is pure; and it does not matter if outwardly everything is impure, yes, if the body is full of sores, scabs, and leprosy.

Blessed are the peacemakers, for they shall be called [the children] of God. (5:9)

With an excellent title and wonderful praise the Lord here honors those who do their best to try to make peace, not only in their own lives but also among other people, who try to settle ugly and involved issues, who endure squabbling and try to avoid and prevent war and bloodshed. This is a great virtue, too, but one that is very rare in the world and among the counterfeit saints. Those who are not Christians are both liars and murderers, as is their father, the devil (John 8:44). Therefore they have no other goal than to stir up unrest, quarrels, and war. Thus among the priests, bishops, and princes nowadays practically all we find are bloodhounds. They have given many evidences that there is nothing they would rather see than all of us swimming in blood. If a prince loses his temper, he immediately thinks he has to start a war. Then he inflames and incites everyone, until there has been so much war and bloodshed that he regrets it and gives a few thousand guldens for the souls that were killed. These are bloodhounds, and that is what they remain. They cannot rest until they have taken revenge and spent their anger, until they have dragged their land and people into misery and sorrow. Yet they claim to bear the title "Christian princes" and to have a just cause.

You need more to start a war than having a just cause. As we have said, this does not prohibit the waging of war; for Christ has no intention here of taking anything away from the government and its official authority, but is only teaching individuals who want to lead a Christian life. Still it is not right for a prince to make up his mind to go to war against his neighbor, even though, I say, he has a just cause and his neighbor is in the wrong. The command is: "Blessed are the peacemakers." Therefore anyone who claims to be a Christian and a child of God, not only does not start war or unrest; but he also gives help and counsel on the side of peace wherever he can, even though there may have been a just and adequate cause for going to war. It is sad enough if one has tried everything and nothing helps, and then he has to defend himself, to protect his land and people. Therefore not "Christians" but "children of the devil" is the name for those quarrelsome young noblemen who immediately draw and unsheathe their sword on account of one word. Even worse are the ones that are now persecuting the Gospel and ordering the burning and murder of innocent preachers of the Gospel, who have done them no harm but only good and have served them with body and soul. We are not talking about these right now, but only about those who claim that they are in the right and have a just cause and think that as high and princely personages they ought not to suffer, even though other people do.

This also means that if you are the victim of injustice and violence, you have no right to take the advice of your own foolish head and immediately start getting even and hitting back; but you are to think it over, try to bear it and have peace. If that is impossible and you cannot stand it, you have law and government in the country, from which you can seek legitimate redress. It is ordained to guard against such things and to punish them. Therefore anyone who does violence to you sins not only against you but also against the government itself; for the order and command to maintain peace was given to the government and not to you. Therefore leave the vengeance and punishment to your judge, who has the command; it is against him that your enemy has done wrong. If you take it upon yourself to wreak vengeance, you do an even greater wrong. You become guilty of the same sin as he who sins against the government and interferes with its duties, and by doing so you invalidate the justice of your own righteous cause. For the proverb says: "The one who strikes back is in the wrong, and striking back makes a quarrel."

Note that this is one demand that Christ makes here in opposition to those who are vengeful and violent. He gives the name "peacemakers," in the first place, to those who help make peace among lands and people, like pious princes, counselors, or jurists, to people in government who hold their rule and reign for the sake of peace; and in the second place, to pious citizens and neighbors, who with their salutary and good tongues adjust, reconcile, and settle quarrels and tensions between husband and wife or between neighbors, brought on by evil and poisonous tongues. Thus St. Augustine boasts that when his mother Monica saw two people at odds, she would always speak the best to both sides. Whatever good she heard about the one, she brought to the other; but whatever evil she heard, that she kept to herself or mitigated as much as possible. In this way she often brought on a reconciliation. It is especially among womenfolk that the shameful vice of slander is prevalent, so that great misfortune is often caused by an evil tongue. This is the work of those bitter and poisonous brides of the devil, who when they hear a word about another, viciously make it sharper, more pointed, and more bitter against the others, so that sometimes misery and murder are the result.

All this comes from the shameful, demonic filth which naturally clings to us, that everyone enjoys hearing and telling the worst about his neighbor and it tickles him to see a fault in someone else. If a woman were as beautiful as the sun but had one little spot or blemish on her body, you would be expected to forget everything else and to look only for that spot and to talk about it. If a lady were famous for her honor and virtue, still some poisonous tongue would come along and say that she had once been seen laughing with some man and defame her in such a way as to eclipse all her praise and honor. These are really poisonous spiders that can suck out nothing but poison from a beautiful, lovely rose, ruining both the flower and the nectar, while a little bee sucks out nothing but honey, leaving the roses unharmed. That is the way some people act. All they can notice about other people are the faults or impurities which they can denounce, but what is good about them they do not see. People have many virtues which the devil cannot destroy, yet he hides or disfigures them to make them invisible. For example, even though a woman may be full of faults and have no other virtue, she is still a creature of God. At least she can carry water and wash clothes.

There is no person on earth so bad that he does not have something about him that is praiseworthy. Why is it, then, that we leave the good things out of sight and feast our eyes on the unclean things? It is as though we enjoyed only looking at—if you will pardon the expression—a man's behind, while God Himself has covered the unpresentable parts of the body and, as Paul says (1 Cor. 12:24), has given them "greater honor." . . .

. . . Learn to put the best interpretation on what you hear about your neighbor, or even to conceal it, so that you may establish and preserve peace and harmony. Then you can honorably bear the title "child of God" before the whole world and before the angels in heaven. You should let this honor draw and attract you; in fact, you should chase it to the end of the world, if need be, and gladly surrender everything you have for it. Now you have it offered to you here and spread out in front of you for nothing. There is nothing that you have to do or give for it, except that if you want to be a child of God, you must also show yourself to be one and do your Father's works toward your neighbor. This is what Christ, our Lord, has done for us by reconciling us to the Father, bringing us into His favor, daily representing us, and interceding on our behalf.

You do the same. Be a reconciler and a mediator between your neighbors. Carry the best to both sides; but keep quiet about the bad, which the devil has inspired, or explain it the best way you can. If you come to Margaret, do what is said of Monica, Augustine's mother, and say: "My dear Margaret, why are you so bitter? Surely she does not intend it so badly. All I notice about her is that she would like to be your dear sister." In the same way, if you meet Catherine, do the same thing. Then, as a true child of God, you will have made peace on both sides as far as possible.

But if you will or must talk about an evil deed, do as Christ has taught you. Do not carry it to others, but go to the one who has done it, and admonish him to improve. Do not act ostentatiously when you come and expose the person involved, speaking when you ought to be quiet and being quiet when you ought to speak. This is the first method: You should discuss it between yourself and your neighbor alone (Matt. 18:15). If you must tell it to others, however, when the first method does not work, then tell it to those who have the job of punishing, father and mother, master and mistress, burgomaster and judge. That is the right and proper procedure for removing and punishing a wrong. Otherwise, if you spread it among other people, the person remains unimproved; and the wrong remains unpunished, besides being broadcast by you and by others, so that everyone washes out his mouth with it. Look what a faithful physician does with a sick child. He does not run around among the people and broadcast it; but he goes to the child and examines his pulse or anything else that is necessary, not to gratify his pleasure at the cost of the child, nor to make fun of him, but with the good, honest intention of helping him. So we read about the holy patriarch Joseph in Genesis 37. He was tending the cattle with his brothers; and when he heard an evil report about them, he went and brought it to their father as their superior, whose task it was to investigate and to punish them because they would not listen to him. . . .

Marty: One line presents two problems. If we can successfully address them, this text will speak to us and our problems in helpful ways. First, what does having a "pure heart" mean? Then, what does it mean to "see" God?

Luther plunges right in with a definition designed to help us. We can picture hundreds of ways to describe a pure heart. "She has such a pure heart," we say of someone who combines activity for others with innocence. Aspiring to be seen as pure-hearted may be the best way not to be pure; one is too busy striving, arranging life in a certain way, cluttering up the mind and heart with agenda items, catalogs, grocery list length "to do" matters, that purity disappears.

The pure heart, for all that, may simply be out of reach from the word go and by definition. One of the psalms that works its way into some liturgies as an Offertory has an individual praying that God would "create a clean heart" and would renew a "right spirit within me." Creation of the pure heart, then, would be God's doing. And the work would never be completed this side of eternity. For a good reason: according to the Bible Jesus was the only human who did not sin, and sin grows out of the impure heart. The rest of us may be declared justified by a loving God who looks not at us but at the Christ in us; yet all the while, we remain at the same sinners, impure.

This word in the Sermon on the Mount is spoken by the one person in history who knows better than any other what is in us. Jesus "knew what was in man," we read elsewhere. So how can he look out at a group of disciples and a little crowd on a mountainside and, beyond them, at the people out of range but not out of mind and find "the pure hearted" ones among them to bless.

Time to call in Luther: To have a pure heart is to have "one that is watching and pondering what God says and replaces its own ideas with the Word of God." That's it. What we say and hear, however true and noble and well-intentioned it will be, will always carry marks of impurity. Purging all that and staying alert for the Word of God when it is uttered and then thinking about it, thus crowding out other thoughts and ideas, is the way to enjoy purity of heart. Count on our commentator to rub it in, this notion that everything is God's work, not ours. He wants us to overlook the scrubbed up, glossy, glistening, iridescent-white berobed monarchs and self-important people, and find purity in the muck.

"A common laborer, a shoemaker, or a blacksmith may be dirty and sooty or may smell because he is covered with dirt and pitch," and yet he will be covered with dignity. Luther pictures him (it could be her) coming out late afternoon, popping open a can of beer or soda, putting his feet on a hassock, arming himself with a remote, sitting back, and watching the last three innings of the ball game. I take that back. The bit about the ball game on television does not work here. Not that Luther had anything against such innocent recreation; he had much for it. But for the present topic he wants the farmer or the worker to sit at home and think.

He will think, as we are encouraged to think, that God has given us what we have—in Luther's case, the family which one gets to support through work. As he does this he may not have the Bible open to Proverbs or Ecclesiastes, but he is "pondering the Word of God in his heart," and is therefore pure. Soot outside, pure incense inside—as we are told to observe him. If such a person's heart is fixed on God, "everything he is and does" is pure for him.

Luther can't resist getting a bit sensual about this. One of his favorite stories about husbands and wives was in Genesis 26:8. It's not my favorite story, the one about Isaac and the men who had their sights on his wife Rebekah. He lied and told them that she was his sister. If they knew she was his wife, they might kill him to pounce on her "because she was attractive in appearance." Now it happened that as a long time passed, Isaac and Rebekah got a bit casual about showing affection in public. The King of the Philistines looked out of the window one day and caught the couple in the act; Abimelech saw Isaac "fondling his wife Rebekah" (Gen. 26:8). You probably know the sequel to that scene so potentially attractive to Hollywood. The King gets angry at Isaac and asks what would have happened had someone "lain with" his wife and thus brought guilt upon all. Hands off, said the King, ordering that anyone who touched the man or the wife would be put to death.

Now that is a supercharged story, but Luther is interested only in a passing detail, a word or two: fondling his wife. He is because he wants to make a point that even in marital sexual activity, so often seen as impure by Christians through history and in his time, God can look at persons and create and see pure hearts. "Nothing can make him impure" who is pondering the Word of God and depending upon God in Christ. "So it is when he looks at his own wife or fondles her, as the patriarch Isaac did," or, in a vice versa that might not have occurred to Luther, "as Mrs. Isaac did" as a cofondler. Now, we read, if the man were to desert his wife or take up with another, he would be going against the commandment of God. Impure.

As we take up the day's works and doings, pondering Luther pondering Isaac can be liberating: however dirty we get in the day's work and play, we can be clean before God. The housemaid who "does her duty and is a Christian in addition," can get dirty from her work but before God "she is a lovely and pure beauty, one that all the angels admire and love to look at." We seem by now to be far from that Offertory prayer, full of churchly language about the clean heart and the right spirit. But that is precisely the point here: go far from the sanctuary, the ritual, the offering. It makes no difference: the pure heart is yours. Luther is so confident about this because nothing God works is impure, and God is working through us today through our efforts at the computer desk, the combine, the classroom, the hospice room.

Now and then Luther steps into the role of church reformer and takes almost gratuitous swipes at the holy people of the church before and in his time. Here he swings at the Carthusians, a religious order dedicated to holiness and pure of heart, and at St. Bernard, also put up as a model. They both had one thing in common, at least one that irritated him the day he spoke and wrote these words. They thought that to be pure you had to be alone, like hermits beyond the monasteries. Bernard contended that whenever he was with people, he defiled himself just by being close to them. Luther really scorns a hermit who said, "The angels cannot come to anyone who moves around in human society," which means, you keep your distance, and I am going to hide.

He cares so much about the idea that one is pure of heart in company, by telling an anecdote about two hermits who would not let their own mother distract and thus impurify them. One day as she kept watch she caught sight of them, so they slammed the door and left her outside crying. In the end they succeeded in persuading her to go away and take comfort that she would see them in the life hereafter. As Luther tells the story, I am not sure he thinks that people who act that way and distort the Word of God that much are going to make it to reunions in that life hereafter. Purity is at home with company, communion, community.

Always eager to teach the difference between a person's role as an individual before God and the same person in some office, he shows how it would defile a person to send someone else to death. But if that person has an "office," in this case a judgeship in a place that has capital punishment, he may send a guilty person to death and not become impure. He will not have violated the Law of God.

Not often ready to speak of rewards, Luther has to here because the Jesus of the Sermon on the Mount did. The pure in heart are blessed by getting to "see God." Here comes another swipe at monks, for he sneers more than he might need to at those who sit in a cell, elevate thoughts heavenward, "leading a 'contemplative life,'" as they call it in their many books. What is going on here? Luther can expound biblical texts that encourage us to be still and know that God is God, to keep silence in the holy place of God, to meditate day and night. His problem is when monks merely meditate, trying to climb up into union with God instead of letting God reach them when they are—at work, being farmers or housemaids, at play, or being lovers.

To "see God," then, is not to have the "vision of God" that the medieval poets and philosophers craved and claimed. To see God means exactly—Luther's word—that one with an open heart learns the will of God and sees not a physical being called God but "sheer, superabundant grace and love." That heart knows what God is like and looks like. Such a person sees the good heart of God. Regard God as angry, and you will not see God correctly. In the Bible, "to see his face" means recognizing the work of God through faith in Christ.

Whoever claims to have seen God head-on is dreaming, making things up, offending the rules of the game that have to do with an encounter with God. There is only one kind of purity that allows one to see God as here described; it is not a purity gained by being alone, contemplating, philosophizing, aspiring, and claiming. The body can be full of "sores, scabs, and leprosy," but the person will be pure in heart if open to God in Christ.

The blessings go on: "Blessed are the peacemakers, for they shall be called children of God" (5:9). As interpreted here, peacemaking is pretty much a one-on-one kind of effort. The disciples and the other poor and pure in front of Jesus as described by Matthew would not have been candidates for an International Commission on Peacekeeping, an arbitration panel, a United Nations or United States (or Judean or Galilean) task force. What we learn here is not against such efforts: peace is peace. But in this interpretation, peacemaking begins at home and next door.

The title "peacemaker" in this case refers to those who try to make peace in their lives and those of others by settling ugly issues, who try to prevent war and bloodshed. In this view, how one deals with a squabbling neighbor connects with how one deals in the face of war. So maybe we are at the edge of commissions, panels, and task forces, which have lessons to learn from the Sermon on the Mount.

Having taken care of hermits a moment before, now Luther takes after hot-headed princes, of whom there were plenty around. "If a prince loses his temper, he immediately thinks he has to start a war." That sounds like reporting on current events in the new millennium. Such a prince inflames everyone. They all fight, many get killed, and then, too late, regret sets in and the prince gives a sacrifice of some money for the souls that were killed. On some occasions Luther bowed, too low, before princes. Here they are "bloodhounds," people of vengeance and anger, extremely negative role models. "Yet they claim to bear the title 'Christian princes' and to have a just cause.

People who start wars on soil influenced by Christianity find it important to bear the title 'Christian prince.'"

Luther, not a pure pacifist and someone who could picture that the office of a ruler might lead one to have to fight a war, here has to deal with Sermon on the Mount language, which is quite limiting to anyone with his viewpoint. He here has to watch and ponder the Word of God, and here is what comes out: "It is not right for a prince to make up his mind to go to war against his neighbor, even though, I say, he has a just cause and his neighbor is in the wrong. (No), the command is: 'Blessed are the peacemakers.'"

Just War theorists—I suppose Luther was one of them in one side of his life, since he inherited language about it—have to confront his words which caution against people using "a just and adequate excuse for going to war" in order to go to war. If the cause is purely defensive, the words of the Sermon on the Mount may be obscured for a moment. But "quarrelsome young noblemen," who have their counterparts that hold diplomatic titles, are "children of the devil," even if they are called Christian. This is strong stuff, but it bids for a hearing.

Even worse, of course, were those who were persecuting the gospel and burning innocent preachers of the gospel. Luther mentions them, and then postpones talk about them for some other day, some other context. Here and now the attack is on the "just cause" claimers.

Tit for tat, eye for an eye, tooth for a tooth, being vengeful and taking revenge were common approaches by victims then and they are now. The victim who gets up and hits back will only heat up and prolong the murderous activity. Law and order man Luther reminds victims that they have governments, from whom they can seek redress. If only that we always do, we might think. He has more faith in the purity of governments than most of us would, but his immediate point rings true. Counter-punching, responding in kind, does not advance the Kingdom of God or advance the status of the person who heats up conflict.

Whoever reads these elements of a conversation does well to engage in self-examination that begins with a critique of one's own taste for hearing gossip. Tell and hear the worst about a neighbor and you will delight your neighbor and increase your status or fame. One dark "beauty spot" on a woman "as beautiful as the sun" will cloud the vision of her in the eyes of many. Let a woman be famous for her honor and virtue, and someone will find something to inspire gossip. To show that people could be trivial in the 16th century as now, listen in to Luther addressing the popular culture instincts and publications of his day. Someone will dig up a story of a lapse to use against a rarely lapsing good person.

Here we get a taste of eloquence: gossips "are really poisonous spiders that can suck out nothing but poison from a beautiful flower." They can notice only impurities in the other. Here also is a stretch: "There is no person on earth so bad that he does not have something about him that is praiseworthy." "If you will pardon the expression," Luther pleads to us, gossips look only at "a man's behind," overlooking the parts of the body God has given greater honor—and covered up.

One of the hardest passages on these pages comes at this point: "put the best interpretation on what you hear about our neighbor," or even hide it from public view. That's all you have to do to hear the word that you will "see God." And then follow that up being a mediator and reconciler among neighbors. If you have to expose someone, do so unostentatiously and not on the pages of a national rumor magazine or post it on the Web. There went the yellow journalism that sustains so many today. If you are offended, follow the rules: talk to the offender; if that fails, talk to someone who has the "office" of listening and judging. A physician deals with a sick child by dealing with a sick child, not by broadcasting word of his infirmity.

Being a peacemaker opens one to a title that Luther thinks any-one should cherish: Children of God. In a world that honors the macho militant, other titles are easier to get. The medals that come with them rust. The title "Child of God" lasts.

For reflection

1. What makes a person "pure of heart"? What does it have to do with the Word?

2. If none but Christ Jesus are truly pure-hearted, how can anyone by Jesus hope to "see God"?

3. How do you respond to the following quote: "Purity is at home with company, communion, community"? Is it possible to be "in the world but not of the world"?

4. Complete this sentence: "A peacemaker is one who . . ."

5. The discussion of peacemaking may lead you to a broader discussion of whether any war is "just" or defendable from a Christian view. However, Luther's words do not point us in that direction. Rather, he makes peacemaking very personal. Who have you known that epitomizes the term, peacemaker?

6. Reflect on the comment: "In a world that honors the macho militant, other titles are easier to get. The medals that come with them rust. The title 'Child of God' lasts."

9

In the Company of the Persecuted

Blessed are those who are persecuted for righteousness' sake, for theirs is the kingdom of heaven.

☙ *Matthew 5:10*

Luther: I have said earlier that all these items and promises must be understood by faith in reference to things that are neither seen nor heard and that they are not talking about outward appearances. How can the poor and the mourners be said to look outwardly successful and blessed when, in addition, they have to suffer all sorts of persecution—all things that the whole world and our reason calls trouble and that they say should be avoided? Therefore whoever wants to have the blessedness and the possessions that Christ is talking about here, must lift up his heart far above all senses and reason. He must not evaluate himself on the basis of his feelings, but he must argue this way: "If I am poor, then I am not poor. I am poor outwardly, according to the flesh; but before God, in faith, I am rich." Thus when he feels sad, troubled, and worried, he must not use this standard and say that he is not a blessed man. But he must turn himself over and say: "I feel sorrow, misery, and sadness of heart; but still I am blessed, happy, and settled on the basis of the Word of God." The situation in the world is the exact counterpart of this, for those who are called rich and happy are not. Christ calls out His "Woe!" against them and calls them unhappy (Luke 6:24, 25), although it appears that they are well off and having the greatest possible success. Therefore they should lift up their thoughts above the riches and fun which they are having and say: "Yes, I am rich and living in the midst of pure fun. But too bad for me if I have nothing else; for there must certainly be plenty of trouble, misery, and sorrow in all this that will come over me before I feel it or know it." This applies to all these items; every one of them looks different before the world from the way it looks according to these words.

So far we have been treating almost all the elements of a Christian's way of life and the spiritual fruits under these two headings: first, that in his own person he is poor, troubled, miserable, needy, and hungry; second, that in relation to others he is a useful, kind, merciful, and peaceable man, who does nothing but good works. Now He adds the last: how he fares in all this. Although he is full of good works, even toward his enemies and rascals, for all this he must get this reward from the world: he is persecuted and runs the risk of losing his body, his life, and everything.

If you want to be a Christian, therefore, consider this well, lest you be frightened, lose heart, and become impatient. But be cheerful and content, knowing that you are not badly off when this happens to you. He and all the saints had the same experience, as He says a little later. For this reason He issues a warning beforehand to those who want to be Christians, that they should and must suffer persecution. Therefore you may take your choice. You have two ways before you—either to heaven and eternal life or to hell, either with Christ or with the world. But this you must know: if you live in order to have a good time here without persecution, then you will not get to heaven with Christ, and vice versa. In short, you must either surrender Christ and heaven or make up your mind that you are willing to suffer every kind of persecution and torture in the world. Briefly, anyone who wants to have Christ must put in jeopardy his body, life, goods, reputation, and popularity in the world. He dare not let himself be scared off by contempt, ingratitude, or persecution. . . .

. . . It is significant that He should add the phrase: "for righteousness' sake," to show that where this condition is absent, persecution alone will not accomplish this. The devil and wicked people also have to suffer persecution. Rascals often get into each other's hair, and there is no love lost between them. So one murderer persecutes another, and the Turk battles against the Tartar; but this does not make them blessed. This statement applies only to those who are persecuted for righteousness' sake. So also 1 Peter 4:15 says: "Let none of you suffer as a murderer or a thief or a wrongdoer." Therefore bragging and yelling about great suffering is worthless without this condition. . . .

See to it, therefore, that you have a genuine divine cause for whose sake you suffer persecution, and that you are really convinced of it so that your conscience can take a stand and stick by it, even though the whole world should stand up against you. The primary thing is that you grasp the Word of God firmly and surely so that there can be no doubt or hesitation there. Suppose that the Emperor, the bishops, or the princes were to forbid marriage, freedom in the choice of food, the use of both kinds in the Sacrament, and the like, and were to persecute you for these things. Then you would have to see to it that your heart is convinced and persuaded that the Word of God has made these things free and unprohibited, that it even commands us to take them seriously and to stake our lives upon them. Then you can have the confidence to say: "This cause does not belong to me but to Christ, my Lord. For I have not concocted it out of my own head. I have not assumed or begun it on my own or at the advice or suggestion of any man. But it has been brought and announced to me from heaven through the mouth of Christ, who never deludes or deceives me but is Himself sheer Truth and Righteousness. At this Man's Word I will take the risk of suffering, of doing and forsaking whatever I should. All by itself, His Word will accomplish more to comfort and strengthen my heart than the raging and threatening of all the devils and of the world can accomplish to frighten me."

Who cares if a crazy prince or foolish emperor fumes in his rage and threatens me with sword, fire, or the gallows! Just as long as my

Christ is talking dearly to my heart, comforting me with the promises that I am blessed, that I am right with God in heaven, and that all the heavenly host and creation call me blessed. Just let my heart and mind be ready to suffer for the sake of His Word and work. Then why should I let myself be scared by these miserable people, who rage and foam in their hostility to God but suddenly disappear like a puff of smoke or a bubble, as the prophet Isaiah says (Is. 51:12, 13): "I, I am He that comforts you; who are you that you are afraid of man who dies, of the son of man who is made like grass, and have forgotten the Lord, who made you, who stretched out the heavens and laid the foundations of the earth?" That is to say: "He who comforts you and takes pleasure in you is almighty and eternal. When it is all over with them, He will still be sitting up there, and so will you. Why, then, let the threatening and fuming of a miserable, stinking bag of worms concern you more than this divine comfort and approval? Be grateful to God and happy in your heart that you are worthy of suffering this, as the apostles went forth (Acts 5:41) leaping for joy over the fact that they were disgraced and beaten down."

These words are a great blessing to us if only we receive them with love and thanks, since we have no shortage of persecution . . . .

So let us be all the more willing and happy to suffer everything. . . . We hear the wonderful and delightful promise here that we shall be well rewarded in heaven and that we should be happy and rejoice over this, as people who do not have to yearn for heaven but already have it . . . . Now tell me whether these simple, short words do not encourage you as much as the whole world can, and provide more comfort and joy . . . . We should not listen to them with only half an ear, but take them to heart and ponder them.

This applies to persecution with deeds and fists, involving person or property, when Christians are seized and tortured, burned, hanged, and massacred, as happens nowadays and has happened before. There is, in addition, another kind of persecution. It is called defamation, slander, or disgrace, involving our reputation and good name. In this way Christians have to suffer more than others. Now Christ discusses this.

Blessed are you when men revile you and persecute you and utter all kinds of evil against you falsely on my account. (5:11)

This, too, is a great and severe persecution and, as I have said, the real suffering of Christians, that they endure bitter slander and poisonous defamation. Though other people must also suffer persecution, violent and unjust treatment, still men are willing to let them keep their reputation and good name. So this is not yet really Christian suffering, which requires not merely all sorts of tortures and troubles, but more; their good name must be spit upon and slandered, and the world must boast loudly that in murdering the Christians it has executed the worst kind of criminal, whom the earth could no longer carry, and that it has done God the greatest and most acceptable service, as Christ says (John 16:2). Thus no name has ever appeared on earth so slanderous and disreputable as the name "Christian." No nation has ever experienced so much bitter opposition and attack by wicked and poisonous tongues as have the Christians.

. . . Anyone who wants to be a Christian should learn to expect such persecution from poisonous, evil, slanderous tongues, especially when they cannot do anything with their fists. He should let the whole world sharpen its tongue on him, aim at him, sting and bite. Meanwhile he should regard all this with defiant contempt and laughter in God's name, letting them rage in the name of their god, the devil, and being firmly persuaded, as we have said above, that our cause is the right cause and is God's own cause. . . . (Before) God our heart and conscience are sure that our teaching is right. We are not teaching on the basis of our own brains, reason, or wisdom, or using this to gain advantage, property, or reputation for ourselves before the world. We are preaching only God's Word and praising only His deeds. . . .

. . . We praise nothing but the Gospel, Christ, faith, and truly good works, and because we do not suffer for ourselves but suffer everything for the sake of Christ, the Lord. Therefore we will sing it to the end. . . .

Rejoice and be glad, for your reward is great in heaven. (5:12a)

These are really sweet and comforting words. They should gladden and encourage our hearts against all kinds of persecution. Should not the dear Lord's Word and comfort be dearer and more important to us than that which comes from a (vile human)? . . . For I hear my Lord Christ telling me that He is truly delighted, and commanding me to be happy about it. In addition, He promises me such a wonderful reward: the kingdom of heaven shall be mine and everything that Christ has, together with all the saints and all Christendom—in short, such a treasure and comfort that I should not trade it for all the possessions, joy, and music in the whole world, even though all the leaves and all the blades of grass were tongues singing my praises. This is not a Christian calling me "blessed," nor even an angel, but the Lord of all the angels, before whom they and all the creatures must kneel and adore. With all the other creatures, therefore, with the leaves and the grass, they must cheerfully sing and dance in my honor and praise.

. . . If every creature, the leaves and the blades of grass in the forest and the sand on the shore, were all tongues to accuse and destroy them, what would all that be in comparison with a single word of this Man? His voice sounds clear enough to fill heaven and earth and to echo through them, silencing the slobbering coughs and the hoarse scratching of His enemies.

You see, that is how we should learn something about using these words for our benefit. They are not put here for nothing, but were spoken and written for our strengthening and comfort. By them our dear Master and faithful Shepherd, or Bishop, arms us. Then we shall be unafraid and ready to suffer if for His sake they lay all kinds of torment and trouble upon us in both words and deeds, and we shall despise whatever is offensive to us, even though contrary to our own reason and heart.

For if we cling to our own thoughts and feelings, we are dismayed and hurt to learn that for our service, help, counsel, and kindness to the world and to everyone we should get no thanks except the deepest and bitterest hatred and cursed, poisonous tongues. If flesh and blood were in charge here, it would soon say: "If I am to get nothing else out of this, then let anyone who wants to, stick with the Gospel and be a Christian! . . ."

. . . Here is what it says: "If you do not want to have the Gospel or be a Christian, then go out and take the world's side. Then you will be its friend, and no one will persecute you. But if you want to have the Gospel and Christ, then you must count on having trouble, conflict, and persecution wherever you go." Reason: because the devil cannot bear it otherwise, nor will he stop egging people on against the Gospel, so that all the world is incensed against it. Thus at the present time peasants, city people, nobles, princes, and lords oppose the Gospel from sheer cussedness, and they themselves do not know why.

So this is what I say in reply to these idle talkers and grumblers: "Things neither can nor should run peacefully and smoothly. How could things run smoothly, when the devil is in charge and is a mortal enemy of the Gospel? There is good reason for this, too, since it hurts him in his kingdom, where he can feel it. If he were to let it go ahead unhindered, it would soon be all over and his kingdom would be utterly destroyed. But if he is to resist it and hinder it, he must rally all his art and power and arouse everything in his might against it. . . ."

. . . We are sure that (enemies) cannot accomplish what they desire until they first topple Christ from heaven and make a liar out of Him, with all that He has said.

For so men persecuted the prophets who were before you. (5:12b)

"When this happens," He wants to say, "you are not alone. Look around, count back to all the holy fathers that ever lived before you, and you will find that their lot was the same. Why should you expect any special treatment? Should He forsake His method for your sake? He had to put up with it when His dear fathers and prophets were persecuted and killed, slandered, and ridiculed by everyone, and made the mockery of the world." As we see from the Scriptures, it had become a common and proverbial expression that if someone wanted to refer to a prophet, he called him a "fool." So in the history of Jehu (2 Kings 9:11), they said of a prophet: "Why did this mad fellow come to you?" And Isaiah shows (Is. 57:4) that they opened their mouths and put out their tongues against him. But all they accomplished by this was to become a terrible stench and a curse, while the dear prophets and saints have honor, praise, and acclaim throughout the world and are ruling forever with Christ, the Lord. "This is what you should expect for yourselves, too," Christ says, "that you will receive the same reward that they did, a reward more abundant and glorious than you can believe or dare to wish. For you are members of the same company and congregation."

What a dear and wonderful Preacher and faithful Master! He leaves out nothing that will help to strengthen and console, whether it be His Word and promise or the example and testimony of all the saints and of Himself. And all the angels in heaven and all the creatures support this. What more would you want and need? With such comfort, should we not put up with the anger and spite of the world and the devil for His sake? What would we do if we did not have a righteous and divine cause, if we had no splendid sayings and assurances like these and still had to suffer, as other people do who have no comfort? In the world it is impossible to avoid all suffering. And for the sake of the Gospel, as we have said, there must be some suffering; it reinforces the faithful and advances them to their promised comfort, joy, and bliss.

Marty: "Blessed are those who are persecuted for righteousness' sake" (5:10). A commentator or spiritual writer has no difficulty, no difficulty at all, speaking to believers in any situation, every circumstance, or most cultures. Only the last two will not find empathic hearers right off. They mention being persecuted, and I have trouble picturing this book falling into the hands of many people in societies where believers are actually persecuted for their faith in Christ.

I wish it were otherwise: otherwise not meaning, of course, that there be more persecuted Christians, but that books like these could reach people in nations where persecution does go on, where the words of the Sermon on the Mount could be comforting. Fortunately, many have these words committed to memory, or they have a few pages of tattered Bibles smuggled to them, so they get comfort through the Word of God. But there is no free flow of information or counsel, because there are persecutors out there. The people with the computers estimate that there are over 160,000 martyrs in the world each year. But, name one. Perhaps we can name two or three who come from North America and get caught passing out Christian literature in a nation that forbids such witness. But we rarely have living contact with those about to be martyred, the truly persecuted.

This is not to say that believers in republics like ours are never snubbed, made fun of, looked down on, spoken ill of. Some find it advantageous to portray themselves as persecutees, pointing to events or signals that they call "anti-Catholic" or "anti-Evangelical" or "anti-Protestant." They picture a world in which everyone is a positive thinker or possibility thinker—where everyone is always nice to everyone else, there is never a bit of intolerance, and everyone is treated with dignity. But against the background of a world where real and systematic persecution goes on, including the world in which the earliest disciples were suffering when the Gospel of Matthew was getting written, most of us live lives of luxury.

Many a pastor in a middle-class community where churchgoing is honored has struggled with biblical texts that talk about the reality of persecution or even that being persecuted is a sign of being truly one of God's own. We have read some sermons that say, in effect, that you are not being persecuted now, but get ready because you will be. But the day does not come, and most of us live out our lives with nothing worse than a few bad public relations smudges, and never a risk to life and limb. So why should we—and this time I include "I" in this "we" without trying to speak for anyone else with assurance—read ourselves into these two final lines of the Beatitudes?

The first way to crack the code of a text is for us to read it, to listen to it. Our two texts are the Sermon on the Mount and Luther's commentary. Luther had it a bit easier than a modern commentator does finding a hearing for this word about persecution. He knew of young men in Belgium killed for preaching the gospel. He was on the run from 1521 to his death in 1546, under equivalents of sentences of death and edicts that licensed anyone to nab him. If truth be told, Luther and Huldreich Zwingli and other reformers who get good marks in many of our books were also themselves on occasion partners in persecutory activities. The Anabaptists, those who rejected infant baptism and rebaptized people when they were adults were particularly offensive. The laws in many places named them blasphemers, and people like Luther, even if a bit reluctantly, in the end agreed with those who turned them over to authorities for the kind of persecution that ends in death.

In these passages, Luther is not holding up the mirror to himself and his colleagues and cobelievers. He is letting them concentrate on the others who would persecute them. "Briefly, anyone who wants to have Christ must put in jeopardy his body, life, goods, reputation, and popularity in the world." What sense does this make in a nation where one could not be elected president or to Congress if he or she made a point of open atheism? What sense does it make if one gets points in professional sports or "Christian Rock" if one is "born again," or at least "spiritual"?

Even more, Luther points to the phrase in the Sermon on the Mount where Jesus is heard adding the phrase "for righteousness' sake." Wryly he notes that even the devil can suffer persecution, but for unrighteousness' sake. It's the same with rascals, murderers, and others who "get into each other's hair" and persecute each other, again as unrighteous. None of that counts. The only condition that gives one bragging and yelling rights is that born of righteous identifications and actions. (That line was a bit unkind: Luther says "bragging and yelling about great suffering is worthless without this condition" of righteousness. He had to be speaking ironically because he was not a booster of boasters.)

Picture this: the emperor, the bishops, or the princes could choose to forbid marriage, freedom of choice of food, the receiving of bread and wine—a controversial issue then—and would persecute you for marrying, eating what you wish, taking the sacrament with both elements. That would be true persecution. The believer would then defy the persecutor: in effect, "I am only doing what Christ told me to do or liberated me to do; it's between you and him, not you and me."

Who cares, we get asked, if a crazy or foolish ruler in his rage threatens Christians? They have Christ "talking dearly" to their hearts. There is no reason to be scared by miserable, raging, and foaming people. They will disappear like a bubble or a puff of smoke. We have the word of Isaiah to back that (Isaiah 51:12, 13.) The eternal God remains with the faithful when all is over for earthly rulers.

In the end Luther does stretch the concept of persecution to include deeds and fists involving person or property just as much as when Christians are seized, tortured, burned, hanged, and massacred, as 160,000 of them will be around the world next year. "Defamation, slander, or disgrace involving our reputation and good name" does hurt, if on a different level and scale. So Christ in the Sermon on the Mount has to say more.

Which leads to the last Beatitude: "Blessed are you when men revile you and persecute you and utter all kinds of evil against you falsely on my account." (5:11). Most of us—or at least I speak for myself—would do anything to shun physical attacks against us as disciples, while we can live with bad words, of which enough get slung around. Jesus in the Sermon on the Mount takes words seriously. Words can ruin lives, can limit opportunities, can stigmatize and harm and kill. All kinds of people can get slandered, but when some are spoken of falsely and derided for Christ's sake, a different order of relations comes into play. It's a new and treacherous game. Luther thinks that no other name matches "Christian" in the ranks of those spoken against and attacked "by wicked and poisonous tongues."

What to do? Show contempt, laugh, defy, invoke God's name when such verbal lashings come. This can be a very short section, since its main points came across in the comment on the verse just above. Sticks and stones and words can hurt alike. But there is always a promise, in the world of Jesus Christ, and as expounded by Luther: "Rejoice and be glad, for, our reward is great in heaven" (5:12a). Here Luther need do no more than tidy things up. Every page has been a call for trust in a God who cares, so the "Amen" at the end only has to reinforce the main idea. Our commentator is derisive and defiant when he speaks of the "slobbering coughs and the hoarse scratching" of enemies. He is speaking of the words of princes and emperors, bishops and popes. Never mind: if they persecute the faithful, they only slobber, cough, and scratch in their throats. All the words of the Beatitudes, we are reminded, are for strengthening and comfort in every circumstance.

It's all a matter of choice. We are advised to sign up with the world's side if we want the world's friendship and not God's. If you are signed up with God, expect comfort.

Oh, yes, there is a postscript, an historical addendum, a footnote of reminder: "For so men persecuted the prophets who were before you" (5:12b). It is often said that Americans are not an historically-minded people. I question that: we do not always have an informed sense of history, but we know just enough to make some commitments or draw some cheer. In this case, the Sermon on the Mount in the last word of the Beatitudes does not say that we will never be persecuted. It says that if persecution comes, we have precedents. None are ranked higher than the prophets of Israel in the counsel of God, so if they suffered, and what they stood for survived, their precedent is to be helpful and reassuring now.

Worth quoting are the final words: "In the world it is impossible to avoid all suffering. And for the sake of the gospel, as we have said, there must be some suffering; it reinforces the faithful and advances them to their promised comfort, joy, and bliss." Luther says that the wonderful Preacher and faithful Master "leaves out nothing that will help to strengthen and console." And there is a valuable question: "What more would you want and need?"

Our ways of life will provide the best answer to that probing inquiry. It's all a matter of trust.

For reflection

1. Have you or anyone you know ever really suffered persecution? How do the words, "for righteousness' sake," change the persecution equation?
2. What is the promise given to those who are persecuted for the faith?
3. What might these passages be saying to those who witness the persecution of others?
4. How is trust tested by persecution? How is your trust in God challenged?

5. The book began with speaking of trust. This theme has been the focus as you wandered through portions of the Sermon on the Mount—commentary on worry and seeking the kingdom, prayer, and the Beatitudes. What have you discovered along the way that has strengthened your faith and solidified your sense of trust?

6. What other question(s) might you wish to pursue with these commentators, provided you could actually sit down and have a conversation?

OTHER LUTHERAN VOICES TITLES

0-8066-4998-4 John McCullough Bade
Will I Sing Again? Listening for the Melody of Grace in the Silence of Illness and Loss

0-8066-4991-7 D. Michael Bennethum
Listen! God Is Calling! Luther Speaks of Vocation, Faith, and Work

0-8066-4992-5 Michael L. Cooper-White
On a Wing and a Prayer: Faithful Leadership in the 21st Century

0-8066-4995-X Barbara DeGrote-Sorensen & David Allen Sorensen
Let the Servant Church Arise!

0-8066-4999-2 Rochelle Melander & Harold Eppley
Our Lives Are Not Our Own: Saying "Yes" to God

0-8066-4596-2 Kelly A. Fryer
Reclaiming the "L" Word: Renewing the Church from Its Lutheran Core

0-8066-4989-5 Ann E. Hafften
Water from the Rock: Lutheran Voices from Palestine

0-8066-4990-9 Susan K. Hedahl
Who Do You Say That I Am? 21st Century Preaching

0-8066-4997-6 Mary E. Hinkle
Signs of Belonging: Luther's Marks of the Church and the Christian Life

0-8066-4996-8 Carolyn Coon Mowchan & Damian Anthony Vraniak
Connecting with God in a Disconnected World: A Guide for Spiritual Growth and Renewal

0-8066-4993-3 Craig L. Nessan
Give Us This Day: A Lutheran Proposal for Ending World Hunger

Large-quantity purchases or custom editions of these books are available at a discount from the publisher. For more information, contact the sales department at Augsburg Fortress, Publishers, 1-800-328-4648, or write to: Sales Director, Augsburg Fortress, Publishers, P.O. Box 1209, Minneapolis, MN 55440-1209.

See www.lutheranvoices.com